Venice Smile.

John C Furey

Acknowledgment

I would like to thank my two amazing sons, Brett and Brandon, for embracing Ellen into our lives at such a young age. I realize it must have been difficult for them at times as so much change occurred during a critical period of their childhood.

I would also like to thank my great friend, Andrew Luke. If not for Andrew, I would never have made the trip to Europe, and would never have had the chance to meet Ellen. Andrew encouraged me, and almost insisted I make the trip to Europe, as I had never been, and he wanted me to experience the wonderful people and cultures. For this, I am eternally grateful.

Contents

Preface

This book is dedicated to my life partner, Ellen Debra Levine. For years, during our many social interactions, Ellen and I would commonly get asked, "How did you two meet?" Upon hearing our story, the response was always the same: "That is so romantic." And quite often, many people would suggest I write a book…….so I did. Though I had never authored a book before and honestly did not know what I was doing, I started by writing down as many details as I could remember. Over many years, on weekends, long flights, and late evenings, I started to piece together the story of how a young, divorced father of two and a young single woman met in Venice, Italy, one September afternoon, had an immediate attraction to one another, and spent the better part of a week traveling through Italy together. Though we had different religious backgrounds, varying political views, and lived 2,000 miles apart, we fell in love and found a way to navigate through multiple life hurdles so we could be together.

While this can be categorized as an autobiography, it is also a wonderful love story, and in many ways, it is a travel journal of my three-week/five-country journey through Europe from Chicago to the Netherlands, France, Switzerland, Italy, and Greece. Additionally, during this time, while checking into a hotel in Naples, Italy, Ellen and I watched on television the horrific attack on our country by terrorists on 9/11. It takes account of how angry and afraid we were and how we managed to find our way through it.

I wanted more than anything to honor my wife by telling our story and to express how fortunate I was to be in St. Mark's Square at the most opportune time. I also hope this story will be an interesting historical reference for our son Ethan, who would not be here today if not for that Venice Smile.

Chapter 1
Crossroads

It was late summer 2001. I was thirty-eight years old and living in the northern suburbs of Chicago, divorced for five years and the father of two young boys. On the surface, life was good for me. I had a promising career working as a middle-level manager for a large insurance company. Although my marriage did not work out, I was very close to my sons Brett and Brandon, who were seven and five years old, respectively. When I got divorced, I moved out and bought a townhome nearby so I could see my boys a couple of evenings during the week and have them stay with me every other weekend as I had joint custody. The boys were close together in age and loved playing together; especially rough like little boys do.

When I was not with my boys or working, I was going through the motions of a painstaking dating scene. Not long after the divorce, I had one serious relationship with a young woman I met at work, which lasted about two years before the relationship ended. She was the one who called it quits; and honestly, I took it hard. Still reeling from the divorce and the abrupt end of the last relationship, I shifted my dating approach to "non-committal" status. I always tried to be nice to the women I dated, took them to nice dinners, sporting events, dancing, etc. However, if things got too serious, I distanced myself as fast as I could. After a while, I just started telling the women I was dating I was not ready for a long-term commitment and only wanted to have fun. In my mind, I probably thought if I was honest about my intentions, it excused me from any responsibility. It did not take long to realize life doesn't work that way, and you cannot play games with people's feelings.

I reflect on one incident with a woman I was dating. I met Michele at the House of Blues in downtown Chicago a few months prior, and started seeing each other on a regular basis. She was a beautiful woman, petite, cute, and very smart. Like my situation, she was divorced and had children. We had much in common and enjoyed each other's company. At times, we even got our kids together and enjoyed taking them to the amusement park or to Chucky Cheese for pizza and games. We even went on vacation together to Puerto Vallarta and had a wonderful time.

One evening, we had just come back from a nice dinner and went back to my place to relax. Out of nowhere, Michelle came close to me, looked me square in the eyes and said, "John, do you want to marry me?" This sudden proposal completely surprised me, and I know from my body language, that I hurt Michele's feelings. I waited for what seemed like forever, but I am sure it was only twenty seconds. I could tell by Michele's facial expression that she was not happy with my hesitation. I responded slowly and softly, "Michele, you know I am not ready for that. We have only been dating a few months. I am not saying I would never consider it, but right now……." Before I could even expand further on my feelings, she collected her things and walked out the door. I never heard from Michele again and I never attempted to contact her; mostly because I knew her decision was final. Of course, I was upset with how our relationship ended so harshly and finally, but I eventually had to come to grips with the fact that Michele and I were at two different points in our lives. I concluded that it was a good thing we did not invest too much more into the relationship. Things went that way for the better part of three years. I would meet someone, date for a period, and then I would end it, or the woman would end it because I could not commit to a meaningful relationship.

The Calling

Three years earlier, I decided I needed a vacation. I was working 50-60 hours per week consistently and realized I could benefit from getting out of town. One day, I stopped at a local travel agency, walked up to the woman at the desk, and said, "Hi, I am interested in going on a singles cruise. I want to meet new people and have a wonderful time." The woman looked at me, smiled, and said, "You don't need a singles cruise, I'm sending you to Club Med." After she explained what Club Med was all about, I got excited and said, "You are right, that's exactly what I'm looking for." Three weeks later, I was on my way to Club Med Turks and Caicos. I went by myself, figuring I would meet people while there and have a fun time. The flight to Turks from Chicago seemed long, with one major connection; and it was extremely late by the time I got to the resort.

After I checked in, I went directly to my room. It must have been around 1 AM. It was customary at Club Med to have guests share a room; a strategy to bring people together. I had not roomed with someone like this since college and was thinking to myself, I hope the guy I am rooming with is not a real jerk. "Oh well, I'm here to have fun - I will deal with it." I opened the door to the room slowly. The room was very dark, but with the light from the hallway, I could see that my roommate was already in bed. I stepped into the room slowly and quietly. Instantly, like a smack in the face, I realized the room temperature was freezing. I could hear the air conditioner cranking away at full speed. Without thinking, I found my way to the thermostat and was in the process of adjusting the air conditioner to warm it up in there when I heard, "What are you doing?"

I said, "Sorry, I did not mean to wake you. Man, it is freezing in here. Do you mind if I warm up just a bit?"

"Actually, I like it cold when I sleep, if you don't mind," stated my new roomie. Tired and not wanting to get off on the wrong foot with my roommate for the first time meeting him, I said, "That's fine."

I thought, "Great, here I am on a tropical island, and I'm

going to have to sleep in a hooded sweatshirt."

As I was unpacking and getting situated, my roommate sat up and told me it was ok to turn on the light if I needed to. We connected immediately and just seemed to fall into one conversation after another and stayed up for another hour getting to know each other. His name was Andrew, a very suave and well-spoken marketing executive from Toronto.

Andrew was a humble man; yet quite confident, and I got the feeling that he was quite accomplished in his field. After talking with Andrew, I realized he was extremely intelligent, and I recall thinking, "This guy is way too sophisticated for me." However, I really enjoyed our conversation, and we ended up spending the week at Club Med hanging out together. Andrew was fun-loving and a great conversationalist. What caught my interest was that Andrew had visited multiple European countries and spoke of his travels with such passion. I had never been to Europe and during one of our deep conversations, Andrew insisted I start planning a trip to Europe; and talked at length about the beauty of the land and the people in Europe.

During the following three years, Andrew and I became best of friends, and went on more singles trips together and always had an exciting time. I could not explain it, but my conversations with Andrew about Europe kept nagging at me, and the thought of going to Europe kept popping into my head like a calling. I dwelled on it, daydreamed constantly about a trip there and subscribed to countless travel magazines. Being divorced, co-parenting my two sons, with little money, I was not exactly sure how I could afford a trip to Europe let alone get the needed time off from work. After months of contemplating this, I started to lay the groundwork for such a trip.

I worked at my company for sixteen years working as a Project Manager in Information Technology. My business was going well; I was in good standing and had a talented team. To pull off a three-week trip to Europe, I knew I first needed to get approval from my boss for the time off. Mark was the Director I was reporting to, one of those young and very smart executives; he focused on business results, of course, but was also very much a family person.

When I told him of the adventure I wanted to pursue, he listened intently. I told him I needed three weeks of vacation to allow enough time to hit all my target destinations. Even though I had ample vacation time, taking three weeks off in a row was outside of the norm for my company, so I really was not sure how Mark would respond. To my surprise, he said, "Well, your shop is in great shape, and I can't see why you wouldn't be able to go." The first step was accomplished. Next, I would need to work things out with my ex-wife. Although we had our differences when we were married, she was very accommodating and said it would be fine. I then started looking for a friend or friends to travel with me. However, my friends were either married, broke, or could not get the time off for such a long trip.

Andrew had met someone incredibly special; and was now in a committed relationship. While I was extremely happy for Andrew, I knew our singles trips together were now over. Well, I was not going to wait any longer and decided to go by myself. As far as financing the trip, I had saved a little money and decided the rest was just going to have to go on the credit card.

For weeks, in the evenings after work and on the weekends, I sat at my computer at home and began planning my trip. I researched destinations, plane and train schedules, hotels, and activities. I continued to seek advice from Andrew, who provided great coaching on attractive destinations. Two specific countries stood out – Italy and France. Italy was a place I had always wanted to go, mostly because my father is full-blooded Italian, and I grew up close to my Italian grandmother. In addition, growing up Catholic, I thought it would be exciting to visit Rome and the Vatican. France was appealing to me because I took eight years of French, four years in high school, and another four years in college.

In high school, I was President of the French Club in my junior and senior years. I loved the French language and minored in it in college. So far, my only opportunity to speak French was when the French Club took our annual trips to Montreal, Ottawa, and

Quebec. Going to France would be something quite special.

After about six weeks of intense planning, I had my itinerary set. I was going to visit five countries in three weeks' time. I would travel light with only a backpack, some cash, and a couple of credit cards. Amsterdam, Paris, Zurich, Venice, Rome, Naples, Athens, and the Greek islands were my target destinations. I initially had Austria and Germany in there, too, but after talking to Andrew, I realized that was a bit ambitious, and had to scale back my trip. After I roughed out how long I would spend at each destination, I booked the train schedules and hotels, and I was ready to go.

At the time I was ready to embark on my big adventure, I had been dating a nice young woman I met at work. Samantha was a real sweetheart, and we had a wonderful time together, but I think both of us realized that it was nothing serious; and we had only been dating a couple of months. When I told her about this trip, she was supportive and upbeat.

One night, when we were out to dinner, about two weeks before I was to depart, Samantha said to me, "John, something tells me you are going to meet your life partner on this trip." I recall laughing aloud at this comment. Although it was five years since the divorce, my mind was nowhere close to thinking about getting married again.

It was the last week of August, and I was almost ready to go.

I just had a few days more before I departed. I purchased a quality backpack and a good pair of walking shoes from a local sporting goods store. The weather was going to be quite warm in Europe in early September, so I did not need heavy clothing. I packed a couple of pairs of jeans, shorts, socks, underwear, and multiple shirts. I figured I would have to do laundry along the way. I said goodbye to my boys. That was a very emotional experience as I had not been away from them for that long and honestly felt a little guilty and selfish about leaving them. They were both extremely sweet, full of smiles and wishing me a good trip – I suspect the result of good coaching from their mother. On Thursday, August 30, I took a taxi to Chicago, O'Hare Airport from there, I flew to New York and then directly to Amsterdam.

On the flight over the Atlantic Ocean, I was so excited I did not sleep one bit; and in fact, stayed up all night reading travel books and studying maps I had purchased in advance.

Amsterdam

I landed in Amsterdam sleep-deprived and groggy; however, the thought of visiting a new country (and three cups of coffee) gave me all the energy I needed to start my adventure. I never had a keen sense of direction; however, with a good map, I am effective in navigating myself around. Amsterdam was unlike any place I had ever seen before. Stunning canals, buildings hundreds of years old with remarkable architecture. Living in Chicago, I was familiar with great architecture, but it was the age of the buildings I found fascinating.

Many of the buildings in Amsterdam were built in the 1600s; and some, in fact, date back as far as the 13th century. The color and unique design of the buildings; especially those right on the canals, decorated with the most beautiful flowers, was something that stopped me in my tracks to just admire and take it all in. The canals were busy with daily commuters and tourists traveling to and from various points in the city. For me, seeing a city with few cars, mostly navigated by bikes and boats, was quite spectacular. My accommodation was modest but comfortable. I was doing my best to keep within budget, so my main criteria for hotels were location, cost, and cleanliness, which the beautiful city of Amsterdam fulfilled. My two-day visit consisted of spending time exploring the local museums (Ann Frank, Van Gogh), countless art galleries, restaurants, and bars.

I had read that Amsterdam had an extremely relaxed and liberal culture. All my interactions with the Dutch were positive. I got the sense the people of Amsterdam were sincerely happy with their lives. A society where they work to live, rather than live to work. Being a young red-blooded American male, it was hard not to notice the beautiful women of Holland. Now, do not get me wrong, there are plenty of beautiful women in the good ole U.S. of A. but this was just entirely different. Tall, short, old, young, and most of them stunningly healthy and beautiful. Growing up in western N.Y. in the small town of Olean, ninety minutes south of Buffalo, I do not recall a lot of middle-aged men or women riding bikes – that was something mostly for children.

However, in Amsterdam, the bicycle was an integrated part of their culture and way of life. The bicycle was their transportation to work and school, running errands, and getting groceries. One does have to be careful where you walk in Amsterdam as it is easy to find yourself stepping in front of fast-moving locals heading to work or school. I lost track of how often I was warned by a bicycle bell to get off the bike path. As I was busy dodging bicycles and riding in every direction, I was determined to check out the legal marijuana phenomenon that I kept hearing about. Marijuana was illegal in the U.S., and I was quite impressed by the little pot cafés sprinkled throughout the city. Even though I was never one to partake in the magical weed, I could not resist stopping in to see what all the fuss was. I went into a "coffee shop," as they call them, and sat down at the bar. On the wall was a blackboard menu that listed every brand of marijuana you could think of – Columbian this, Hawaiian that. On the bar, there were rolling papers conveniently located for your pleasure. I did not stay long other than to have a cup of excessively strong coffee, but it was honestly quite amusing and an excellent venue for people-watching.

The service in all the restaurants I visited was pleasant and friendly. I never had an issue, though I did not speak the language, an indication Amsterdam gets a lot of tourists from all over the world. I found the food in Amsterdam to be delicious and unique.

During the afternoon, rather than pick a specific restaurant, I just quickly visited various little places I found while walking. Bitterballen was a new positive experience for me, which is a little beef or veal appetizer treat. I am not a big red meat eater but these I just had to try. Another delicacy that stood out was the herring – everywhere I turned, people were enjoying raw herring. I did pass on that experience although it is quite healthy.

Amsterdam has the most amazing cheese shops. I took time out to visit multiple cheese shops to sample the many diverse types of cheese and listen to the local proprietors talk about their history. For dinner, I stopped at a quaint little restaurant with mostly locals and enjoyed the best goulash I have ever tasted (all due respect to Grandma Furey). Next onto what the Dutch are very well known for – and that is chocolate that will make your head spin. Now sweets, especially chocolate, are my weakness. I have a lot of discipline in most aspects of my life, but when it comes to Dutch chocolate, I just cannot be trusted. I used every bit of self-control to take only a few samples from the shops I visited.

Venice Smile for Ellen

As it was now starting to get late, my curiosity eventually got the best of me, and I had to meander my way over to the infamous Red-Light District. My preconceived notion of the district could not have been more incorrect. I envisioned a rundown, disgusting area where older prostitutes sat in decrepit buildings (with, of course, little red lights in the window) and waited for pathetic old men to visit. To my surprise, I saw blocks and blocks of beautifully decorated buildings with the most gorgeous young women from every ethnic background you could imagine proudly displayed in huge bay windows.

Both men and women were lined up outside, either just browsing or waiting their turn for a little meet and greet. When an eager patron visited one of the women, you would see the window curtains close and then reopen a little later, when finished with their conversation, of course. I did not partake in that experience either, but it was certainly interesting to observe. As I walked through the district, I also noticed establishments where they had live strip and sex shows. These were actual places where you could go in and sit down, order a beverage, and watch people have sex. I thought to myself that I had better head back to my hotel before I got myself in trouble. Once I got to my hotel, I was quite exhausted and went right to bed after a (cold) shower.

My second day in Amsterdam was to visit some of the popular museums. From my travel research, I knew I needed to visit the Ann Frank House. Anne Frank was a thirteen-year-old Jewish girl who went into hiding during the German occupation of the Netherlands during World War II.

Anne and her family hid from the Germans in a secret area above the business where Anne's father had worked. While in hiding, young Anne wrote in her diary about her experiences. For more than two years, Anne and her family endured the hardships of living hidden away in isolation before being discovered and captured. Tragically, Anne, her sister Margot, and her mother all died in camps months after being discovered. Only Anne's father, Otto, survived and was liberated by the Russians after the war.

Later, one of the women (Miep Gies) who helped hide the family gave Anne's diary and notes she kept while they were in hiding to Otto. The father later published Anne's diary. The place where Anne and her family hid from the Germans is now a museum you can visit in Amsterdam. As I walked through the museum, I was moved with emotion by Anne's story. I thought to myself, "What an exceptional young girl." Her story is both a tragedy and an inspiration. The rest of my final day in Amsterdam was spent walking the beautiful streets and visiting the amazing squares. Truly a beautiful city, and I knew I would someday return.

Chapter 2

Paris

After enjoying my last day in beautiful Amsterdam, I packed up my gear and headed to Amsterdam Central train station. In my attempt to make the most efficient use of my time, I decided I would take the night train to Paris. I had never taken a night train before, so this was going to be an entirely new experience for me. I was trying to keep expenses down, so I arranged a slow-moving train, one that would take most of the night to get there. Knowing that I really have a tough time sleeping sitting up, I reserved one of those sleeper cabins on the train. I wanted to be fresh to start my first day in Paris. The train pulled out late from Amsterdam, but I stayed awake another couple of hours, as I was anxious; I was finally going to see beautiful France.

When it was time for bed, I headed to my sleeper cabin. It was one of those deals where you slide the door open to a tiny little cabin with bunk beds on the left and right side with the outside window in the middle. To my surprise, when I arrived, no one else was in the cabin, and it looked like three other sleeper slots besides mine were empty , maybe I caught a break and will have the entire cabin to myself.

I climbed up to the second-tier bed and started to settle in. During my research and planning for the trip, I observed ample caution about tourists targeted in Europe by thieves and pickpockets. So, being ever so cautious, I padlocked my backpack to the bed rail and made sure there was no easy access to any of the zippers. I was spooning with my backpack. I am sure I looked silly, but I did not care. I put my credit cards and what little cash I had in one of those travel pouches, hung it around my neck, and tucked it down into my pants – not wonderfully comfortable. If someone tried to rob me, it was not going to be easy. I then went to sleep. It must have been about ninety minutes later when the cabin door opened, and a family of four came in, which woke me up instantly.

It was about 1:30 AM by this time, and the family did not even attempt to be quiet or considerate. "You have to be kidding me," I mumbled to myself. Although it was quite dark, it looked like a father, mother, and two children younger than six years old. The parents put the kids to bed, and it seemed like the kids and mother went right to sleep. The father never went to sleep and kept leaving the cabin and coming back in. I do not know if he went out to smoke or enjoy a cocktail or what, but just as I would fall back asleep, he would open the door again and wake me up. Naturally, I am a non-confrontational person, so I did not say anything to the man even though I was quite perturbed that, once again, I was in for a sleepless night. The man did not seem to care if he bothered me or not.

I think it may have been around 6 AM when the train pulled into Paris du Nord train station. All my cabinmates, including the father, were sleeping. I quickly got my backpack in order, made as much noise as I could, slammed the cabin door, and jumped off the train with a gratifying smirk.

Although exhausted, my adrenaline started flowing – after all, I was in Paris! It was early Sunday morning, the streets were empty, and very few stores or even coffee shops were open. The area around the train station was run down with trash blowing down the street, buildings vandalized by graffiti, and homeless spread out over various areas. It was an overcast sky, and it was very gloomy yet warm. "This really is not how I imagined Paris," I thought. I obviously did not do my homework because I had absolutely no clue where my hotel was. I thought I would just figure it out as I went along. Therefore, I pulled out my handy dandy Paris Street map that I purchased back in Chicago; and that was absolutely no help.

After walking around a bit, I spotted a local man casually walking down the street, enjoying a cigarette. He was a slender man, about five feet, seven inches tall, wearing jeans and a wrinkled sports coat; his hair was disheveled, and he had a beard growth of about three days. I was not sure if he was just coming home from a night out or was just starting his day.

Anyway, he seemed harmless enough, so I walked up to him, anxious to see how effective my high school and college French was going to be in Paris (it had been a good eighteen years since I attended a French class). Well, to my surprise, when I approached the Frenchman, he was quite delightful. His name was Rene, and he seemed intrigued, almost delighted to be talking to an American, even though it was a sleep-deprived American, speaking French poorly and completely lost. With my broken French and his broken English, I was able to get across to him that I was lost and trying to find my hotel, which I knew to be located near Notre Dame. My high school French teacher, Mr. Paul Hessney, would be proud. In French, Rene explained that my hotel was far away and it would be easier if he could just take me there.

At first, I said that would be too much bother, but I quickly assessed this little man was not taking no for an answer, so I agreed. He stated, however, that we would first drop by his apartment so we could get coffee. Feeling tired from the man on the train keeping me up all night, deep down, I was thinking, "I just want to get to my hotel and get a little shut-eye." However, I then realized I was there for the cultural experience and adventure. Off Rene and I went down the street, chatting away. After a couple of blocks, we arrived at his apartment, which was on the third floor of a modest building.

Since I was eleven years old, I trained heavily in martial arts, earning my black belt at an early age. Over the years, I became an instructor and had my own martial arts studio as a side business. It was my passion and something I loved to do. By the time of this European adventure, I was an accomplished martial artist, in decent shape, and was confident in my ability to defend myself. During the entire time I was walking up the three flights of stairs and into this stranger's apartment that I just met on the street moments ago, I was anticipating an ambush or a mugging and was contemplating how I would defend against various scenarios. I kept my hands and feet ready to go in case something happened. I was ready for anything.

Fortunately, when we got into his apartment, no one else was there. His apartment was simple yet nicely decorated and maintained. He lived alone, and I soon discovered that he was a university professor (although I never assessed which university or what subjects he taught). As Rene made his way to the kitchen to brew the coffee, I put my backpack in the corner and had a seat on his couch.

A few moments later, Rene served me a freshly brewed hot cup of coffee and then excused himself to use the bathroom. Being ever so cautious, I thought about a case just ten years prior where a deranged man in Milwaukee poisoned, killed, and mutilated countless men and boys. Believe me. No one was going to poison, kill me, and stuff me in a cargo trunk. As soon as Rene left the room, I got up, ran into his kitchen, and poured the coffee down the sink. I did feel bad about it, but I just could not take any chances, especially since I could not see him as he made the coffee.

As soon as Rene returned, we engaged in idle small talk, and he said he was going to make a call. I chuckled to myself because although he was speaking quite fast and I was only picking up bits and pieces of what he was saying, I was able to make out that he was explaining to his friend that he met this crazy American near the train station, and I was visiting for coffee.

Once his call was over, I asked him in French if he would be able to take me to my hotel now ("Pouvez-vous s'il vous plaît m'emmener à mon hôtel maintenant?"). He said of course but first we would have to stop at the local coffee shop because all his friends wanted to meet me ("Oui bien sûr, mais nous allons d'abord vous présenter à mes amis".) I chuckled to myself as I realized I might never get to my hotel at this rate. Rene was such a delight; it was hard for me to say no, so I decided to go with the flow, and off we went.

We walked another five blocks or so and arrived at a genuinely nice coffee shop. This was for locals, as I got the impression I was the only tourist in the restaurant. As we walked in, it was obvious Rene's friends were already there sitting at the bar. I surmised when I first met Rene, he was on his way to meet his friends for breakfast. There was a man and two women, and they were just as friendly as Rene and genuinely glad to meet me. I am quite certain I was the only one in the place who was not smoking, and it was difficult to breathe. It was also quite noisy in the coffee shop, so it was difficult for me to understand everything they were saying as none of them spoke any English. However, my French was at least good enough to exchange some pleasantries.

They introduced themselves as Elsa, Suzanne, and Jean. They all had a good laugh when I said with the worst possible accent, "Mon nom est Jean aussi." I remember telling them I was from Chicago. Of course, that is when they did demonstrate the only English they knew by saying "Bang, bang……Al Capone" while using their fingers as guns. Well, we did have an exceptionally good visit together, and this time, I enjoyed a nice cup of coffee, and the freshest croissant one could ask for. In true American fashion, I bought them all their breakfast, and after about an hour, Rene was finally going to honor his commitment to take me to my hotel. I said "Au revoir" to my new friends, and after multiple handshakes and hugs, I followed Rene out the door, hopefully this time in the direction of my hotel.

Rene did exactly what he said he would do. He escorted me back to the train station, bought my ticket for me, and waited with me for the right train. The train arrived, and we jumped on. Being from a small town, I was not experienced riding the subway (Metro), so I was glad Rene was there to make sure I did not end up in Versailles. It seemed like it took a while to arrive at the station that dropped us off near Notre Dame, but that may have only been in my mind. I had given Rene the address to my hotel, and he seemed to know where it was.

On our way, we walked by the beautiful and infamous Notre Dame Cathedral, and I could tell Renee was proud to be the person to first show me this historic landmark. Raised Catholic, attended Catholic school, I was immediately in awe of the grandeur of the cathedral.

We walked about ten minutes more and ended up right in front of my hotel. I was so happy to have arrived. With my lack of sleep, I was almost giddy. I felt so grateful for Rene's generosity; I reached into my pocket and offered to pay Rene (I think it might have been about $40 U.S. dollars). Rene's face quickly turned serious, and he said, "No m'insultez pas." I was letting my ignorance of European culture show through, and I immediately knew I made a mistake. However, I quickly rebounded, put my money away, and gave Rene a genuine handshake and hug. His frown changed back to that most wonderful smile, and he handed me a little piece of paper that had his name and phone number on it; and he quickly walked away. Just like that, he was gone.

You see, all this time when I thought he might try to take advantage of me, might attempt to mug me or even kill me, he was just a wonderful human being, anxious to expand his horizons and help someone in need. For years, I had heard about how rude the French people are to Americans; that, in fact, they hate Americans. Yet my very first experience could not have been any more pleasant. Here is a man who took a lost American into his home, offered him coffee, then proudly introduced him to his friends before personally escorting him to his hotel, a good hour out of his way roundtrip. I wondered if I would help someone visiting from another country, lost in downtown Chicago? Probably not. It was a great life lesson for me.

I checked into my hotel, a boutique-style place with a small lobby. A friendly front-desk manager with a sincere smile immediately greeted me. I must have looked very non-French because he immediately addressed me in English.

After an incredibly fun but exhausting morning with Rene and his friends, I was relieved I did not have to struggle with French while checking in. I had to leave the clerk with my Passport, which I hated to do, but knew it was customary in Europe. I was then presented with an old-fashioned key and pointed up the staircase.

My room was on the second floor, in the far back corner of the hotel. The view was nothing to write home about, but honestly, at that point, I just wanted to find the bed and grab a little nap before exploring the city of Paris. I quickly changed into gym shorts and a tee shirt and fell fast asleep. When I awoke, it was close to 2:00 PM. I was still quite exhausted but knew I needed to wake up and get myself out the door.

I jumped in the shower, brushed my teeth, quickly changed into street clothes, and off I went. My first stop was going to be

Notre Dame, which I recalled was close to the hotel. As I started walking towards the cathedral, a man was in the middle of the sidewalk on his knees in a prayer position, and he had a sign that read "J'ai faim" which means I have hunger.

His clothes were torn and dirty, his hair and beard knotted. I was certainly no stranger to running into homeless, but this hit me in the heartstrings, and I reached into my pocket and dropped what was equivalent to $10.00 in American currency into his hat that he had placed out in front of him. Other than a slight nod and a quick closing and opening of his eyes, he never moved or showed any emotion. I slowly walked around the manand kept going along the boulevard.

The Cathedral of Notre Dame is huge, and you can see it from quite a distance before you get to it. It was majestic and awe-inspiring. You cannot help to be impressed with the two huge towers on the left and right and a huge circular stain-glass window design in the middle.

Before my trip and on the airplane, I researched Notre Dame. The Cathedral has a rich and interesting history. Construction of the cathedral started in the twelfth century and was completed over a two-hundred-year period; its official opening was in 1345. Over its eight-hundred-year history, it was chosen by kings and emperors as the location for their crowning. Even the great Napoleon chose Notre Dame as the location of his crowning in 1804. The cathedral has survived the French Revolution, World War II, and many fires. Over the centuries, Notre Dame underwent needed renovation and repair.

As I approached the front of the cathedral, I could see crowds of tourists in every direction. "I guess I'm in the right spot," I thought to myself. As I walked into the front entrance, I was overcome with emotion. The pictures I had seen in the travel books did not do it justice. It was ornately decorated, with huge pillars and archways. It reminded me of St. Mary's Basilica in my hometown of Olean, New York, only on a more grandiose scale. I decided not to take a guided tour and figured I would just walk through it and take it all in. It was a beautiful experience. I think I may have been there an hour or so before I decided I would see other areas of Paris.

My next destination was going to be the Eiffel Tower. I knew it would be much faster to take the Metro, but I figured that if I walked the beautiful Seine River, I would get to see more of the sites. Using my Paris Street map, I charted a course and off I went. According to the map, it looked like it was going to be less than a two-mile walk. During my walk, I enjoyed watching the Parisians go through the normal motions of their lives. I was simply happy to be there and felt blessed to experience the great French culture.

Eiffel Tower

Like what I experienced at Notre Dame, you see the Eiffel Tower long before you get to it. I mean, come on, how can you miss it? It is over one thousand feet tall and is one of the most recognized structures in the world.

The tower was named after the architect who designed and built it in 1889, Gustave Eiffel. I was so excited that before I got in line to go up into the tower, I decided I would make a call to my parents. It was now early afternoon, so even with the six-hour time difference between Paris and New York, they should be awake by now.

I found a local bank of phones, used my prepaid card, and dialed my parents. My father picked up the phone right away. I said, "Dad, you are never going to guess where I am."

My father was always excited for me, and I heard him say to my mother, "Hold on, it's John." Then he said very excitedly, "Johnny, where are you now"?

I said, "Dad, I'm standing right in front of the Eiffel Tower."

My father was extremely happy for me and just said to enjoy myself and to be careful. I did not stay on the line long, told my dad I loved him and said good-bye. This may sound a little silly, but it was an emotional moment for me talking to my dad from the Eiffel Tower, as I knew my dad was proud of me.

I loved my parents very much, but I was closer to my father. Both my parents had modest upbringings. My mother, daughter of a coal miner, was from a very small town in northern Pennsylvania and quit high school in the tenth grade. My father, eight years older than my mother, was raised in my hometown of Olean, New York, a small but adorable town (population ~14,000), sixty miles south of Buffalo.

Dad, or "pops" as I call him, was a very mild-mannered, full-blooded Italian with a strong work ethic. My parents met at a bingo game when my mother was sixteen. They were married one year later. Growing up, my mother was head of the household and the primary disciplinarian. My dad, a selfless man, always went along with the flow and catered tirelessly to my mother, my sister, and me. My dad worked during the day as a bench grinder in a local knife factory, Cutco Corporation (Alcas). At night, he worked as a cook in an Italian restaurant called The Castle. My mother was a meat wrapper at Reid's grocery store during the day. When I was younger, my paternal grandmother would babysit. As much as my father worked, he never missed any of my school functions, band concerts, football games, or martial arts tournaments. He was always in the audience or on the sidelines, cheering me on. That always meant so much to me.

I was anxious to get on with the tour. For some reason, the line waiting to go up the tower was not too bad. After thirty minutes or so of waiting in line and a stop at security, I was able to take an elevator to the second floor of the tower. The view from the elevator on the ride up was magical. When the elevator door opened on the second floor, the first thing I noticed was the tourists from all over the world enjoying this great landmark.

There were shops and places to eat, as well as the actual office of the tower's builder, Gustave Eiffel. Then, of course, there was the amazing view. It seemed like I could see all of Paris. I walked all around the observation deck, taking in every view possible. I was in Paris, and I was on the top of the Eiffel Tower. I felt a sense of accomplishment as if I had achieved a lifelong dream.

I took a moment to reflect and again thought of my dear friend Andrew Luke, who encouraged me to make this trip. I wished he were there with me but understood that he met his beautiful life partner Julia and was enjoying his life in Oakville, Ontario.

I walked all around the circumference of the tower, stopping to peer out at the magnificent city of Paris. I was in awe of the pure beauty of my surroundings. As I attempted to better understand all the impressive buildings in my view, I observed maps made available on the tower platform. The very first thing that caught my attention was the world-renowned Seine River, which flowed right by the tower, active with passenger cruisers taking tourists down the Seine. Just over the Seine due west, I could see a striking structure, which I identified as the Palais de Chaillot, a huge wing-shaped group of buildings that contained a naval museum surrounded by beautiful gardens. I learned the French take great pride in their gardens and fountains, a passion that dates to the time of Louis XIV.

From the eastern side of the tower, I got a great look at the Parc du Champ De Mars, a gorgeous and expansive green area that spans from the base of the tower all the way to Ecole Miliataire (military training facility). This huge park, a tribute to the Roman God of war, is where Parisians and tourists lounge, socialize, and admire the views. Northeast of the park is Invalides containing monuments and museums. I was so enthralled by the Eiffel Tower, I could literally spend all day there, but I knew that I had much more to see and experience. Off in the distance, just over one mile to the north, I could see the Arc de Triomphe, which was next on my list of places to visit. I made my way to the elevators and returned to street level.

The Arc de Triomphe

The Arc de Triomphe was less than a mile and a half away. Though there were several bus and metro options, I decided I would walk. I was not in a hurry and just wanted to experience the city. It was a warm and sunny day but a very comfortable temperature. Once I crossed over the Seine River, I walked at a nice leisurely pace. Somehow or another, I ended up on the Champs-Elysees, where I could plainly see the massive structure of the Arc from a great distance.

In total, it only took me about thirty minutes to get to the Arc. While I was walking, I recalled seeing old footage of Germans marching through the archway during the German occupation of Paris during World War II, which gave me the chills. The structure is unique in that it serves as the center of twelve different avenues that extend out from the Arc like spokes in a wheel.

As I approached the impressive structure, I could see the monument sitting in the center of a huge roundabout with cars, buses, and scooters buzzing all around it, heading in all directions. How the hell am I supposed to get to it, fly, I mumbled to myself. It took me a few minutes to figure out that to get to the entrance of the arc, I had to pass down into an underground walkway, which took me underneath the street and then up again to the structure.

As I emerged from the underpass, I was in awe of the massive structure and impressive design of the Arc. The outside walls of the monument display the names of the military men and women who lost their lives in wars defending France. I walked around and under the Arc and was interested in finding The Tomb of the Unknown Soldier from World War I. An eternal flame has burned at the tomb since 1920 to memorialize soldiers lost in war defending France.

Once inside, I spent time reading about the history of the Arc. The Arc de Triomphe built from 1806-1836, honors the French soldiers who died in wars dating back to the French Revolutionary War. It is a huge monument, which stands 164' high and is 148' wide.

I then climbed the spiral staircase to the roof. On the top of the structure, I had an amazing 360-degree view of the city. The first thing I noticed, of course, was the amazing Eiffel Tower where

I had just been. It was truly a grand site from the Arc standing there in all its glory.   I spent some time trying to identify some of the other points of interest. The Champs-Elysees was heavy with traffic in every direction. It was impressive to see and feel the energy of this great city. With a little help from my street map, I could identify The Louvre, Notre Dame, and the beautiful domes of the Sacre-Coeur Basilica.

Upon taking in the view, I saw a pretty, young woman standing next to the wall peering out at the city. She seemed deep in thought and had a welcoming demeanor, as if she was thinking about how beautiful Paris is. No one was with her, and she looked about my age, maybe a little younger. I had been in Europe a few days now, and I had not even thought about meeting a potential romantic partner.

I decided to walk in her direction, and as I got closer, she looked over at me, pleasing but not necessarily inviting. I decided I would ask her if she was a tourist. She was very nice and introduced herself as Lori from Green Bay, Wisconsin. She was visiting Paris for the first time and was just enjoying some of the landmark sites. For a brief second, I thought I would ask her to have coffee or a glass of wine, but after we exchanged a few more pleasantries, I wished her well in her travels, and I headed towards the exit. I guess I just was not feeling a connection, and she seemed fine to let me be on my way.   I returned to the Champs-Elysees and started walking.

I decided not to use my map and headed east.   It was the most impressive boulevard I had ever seen. There was an abundance of high-end shopping and restaurants, as well as what looked like residences of the super-wealthy. I often would just stop at the beautiful windows and admire the creative displays. I knew I could not afford to shop in any of those stores, so I just kept walking. Since it was Sunday, the streets were packed with tourists exploring. Open-air tour buses were running in every direction, and locals on scooters weaved in and out of traffic at extremely high speeds. Street cafes were busy with patrons enjoying a great meal, a coffee, or a glass of wine.

I walked all the way to Jardin des Tuileries, beautiful gardens that were designed by King Louis IV's landscaper. I was taken back by the Parisians, young and old, enjoying the beauty of the gardens. Lovers of all ages strolled hand and hand or could be seen kissing on a park bench.

There were beautiful ponds where the sun glistened off the surface, and drafts of ducks were leisurely making their way through the water. It seemed as if the gardens were a place where the locals would come to feed the pigeons as they were flying every which way. It really was quite beautiful, and I smiled as I thought it would be so nice to share this with a romantic partner. While I was certainly happy and most fortunate to be on such a trip, admittedly, I was feeling a little lonely.

It had been a very long day, and I was starting to get tired and hungry. After all, I visited three major tourist destinations in a single day (Notre Dame, Eiffel Tower, and the Arc de Triomphe). I wandered my way through the gardens exited the gardens to the north, and stumbled upon a quaint area called Saint Honore.

I believe I was on the main street, Rue Saint Honore, which had beautiful shops, hotels, and restaurants. Since I was not spending a lot on breakfast or lunch, I decided I was going to treat myself to a nice dinner.

The great thing about restaurants in Paris is they proudly display their menus out front. I visited multiple restaurants and read each of the menus. I selected a restaurant that had a great menu but was not too pricey. I went in and was greeted by a very formal host who escorted me to a small table near the front of the restaurant where I could peer out the window and watch all the locals passing by. It dawned on me that I was having French food for the first time in my life. The waiter either did not speak English or refused to, and my French was rusty. I did not really understand what I ordered exactly, but when the food arrived, everything was beautifully prepared and tasted fantastic. I figured out I had ordered an amazing veggie stew called Ratatouille. It really was delicious, but the portions the French provide are small compared to what you get in America. I was still hungry, so I ordered an amazing crème Brule for dessert and washed it down with a beer.

After dinner, I flagged down a taxi and had him take me back to my hotel. It did not seem like it took very long to get to the hotel, so I must not have been too far away.

Once back to my hotel, I rested on the bed and dozed off for a brief catnap. After about two hours, I was ready to go, jumped in the shower, put my best dress clothes on and went down to the lobby to greet the concierge. I knew Paris had great nightlife, but I had not researched which clubs were popular. I asked the concierge, who was quite helpful.

He wrote down the name of a club on a piece of paper and told me to just hand it to the taxi driver, and they would know where to go. Taxis were easy to flag down in Paris. I literally just stepped into the street and raised my hand, and a driver appeared. In about ten minutes, we pulled up to this lively club. There were young men and women standing out front smoking or just talking. The line to get in was about twenty deep, where two huge bouncers at the entrance of the club randomly selected whom they let into the club.

After about twenty minutes, I found myself at the head of the line. One of the very large bouncers just looked down at me and grimaced. I had a feeling there was no way in hell I was getting into this club, so I thought I better think of something. I quickly reached into my pocket and collected what would have been about twenty-five dollars in US currency, shook his hand, and discreetly deposited the money in his palm. After all, I'm Italian, and we tip for everything. Not sure what his reaction would be, he removed the rope barrier and waived me in.

As I entered the club, a smile immediately came over me as I could literally feel the bass from the sound system vibrate my internal organs. The music was blaring. People were on the dance floor moving in all directions – it was a party. I weaved my way through the club, elbow-to-elbow, and competed with others to get to the bar or a drink.

I was used to this scene as the nightlife in Chicago is quite spectacular. I wedged my way in between a couple of women sitting at the bar, raised my hand with some cash, and quickly flagged down the bartender, who promptly provided me with the bottle of beer I had requested. I was all set now to do some serious people-watching. I glanced around the room periodically to see if any of the beautiful French women were looking my way.

I had learned somewhere along the way (probably from my friend Andrew), that if women are interested in you, they would be the ones to establish eye contact. Well, no one was establishing eye contact with me, so I just decided I would just sit back, enjoy the music and dance a little by myself. From my years of martial arts experience, I was always quite flexible and nimble on the dance floor and loved to dance. When a great song would come on, out to the dance floor, I went by myself, beer in hand. I did not really care if I looked funny. No one knew me in Paris anyway. I had a very nice time even if I was by myself.

Although the French women were quite gorgeous, I didn't see anyone I would want to spark up a conversation with. A couple of hours and several beers later, I decided I had experienced enough of the Paris nightlife and grabbed a taxi back to my hotel. I knew I had a busy day of exploring ahead of me and wanted to get some sleep. I settled into my comfy bed and fell deep asleep quite amazed I was in Paris.

Sacre Coeur

On Monday, I awoke very early and was feeling refreshed. It would be my last day in Paris, and I wanted to see as much as I could in one day.

I showered, dressed, and headed down to the small breakfast area off the lobby of the hotel. I woofed down a croissant and a cup of coffee and headed out the door. I decided I would venture over to the Basilica de Sacre Coeur de Montmartre, a gorgeous Roman Catholic Basilica now declared a national monument. After talking to the front desk clerk, I discovered I could get there relatively easily and at a low cost via the metro.

After a short walk, I found the metro entrance and surprisingly figured out how to use the ticket machine. At first, I was a little nervous I would get on the wrong train heading in the wrong direction, but surprisingly did everything correctly. After a number of stops, approximately twenty-five minutes, I arrived at my destination.

Upon first seeing Sacre Coeur, I was astonished by its magnificence. The structure sat high on a hill overlooking all of Paris, is a beautiful light color, with a huge dome that soars high in the sky complimented by four smaller domes.

Upon touring the basilica, I learned about its historical significance; built between 1875 and 1914 and dedicated to the sacred heart of Jesus Christ. The interior of the basilica was stunningly lavishly decorated, and an impressive altar under a monstrous dome with an eye-catching painting of Jesus with outreached arms. The stained glass windows throughout were impressive and transported me back in time to when I was a young boy attending Sunday mass in my hometown.

A group of nuns, perhaps on a pilgrimage, were all kneeling in the front of the basilica, deep in prayer. I peered around and noticed the beautiful glow of candles being lit by visitors in memory of their loved ones. I paused for a moment and said Hail Mary and Our Father.

After about 45 minutes of touring the basilica, I headed to the subway station, this time targeting The Louvre as my destination.

The Louvre

When I arrived at the Louvre, I was impressed by the characteristic pyramid design of the famous museum's exterior. I was happy I got there early because the lines to get in were already quite long. I got in line and waited patiently. I think it must have been about an hour before I got in. I guess Mondays weren't the best day to go, but I didn't have much choice since I was leaving for Switzerland early the next morning.

I would never characterize myself as knowledgeable about fine art; however, I did take an entry-level art class in college and recall lectures covering the most famous artwork displayed in The Louvre.

I spent more than two hours in the museum and had the good fortune to see Leonardo Da Vinci's Mona Lisa and The Virgin Of The Rocks, Caravaggio's Death of a Virgin, Jacques-Louis David's Coronation of Napoleon, Eugene Delacroix's Liberty Leading the People, and Rembrandt's Supper at Emmaus, just to name a few. The Louvre also contained artifacts from ancient Greece, Rome, and Egypt. There was so much to see. I was quite overwhelmed by it all. I knew I would return one day to spend more time and fully appreciate the grandeur of what the museum had to offer. Upon leaving the museum, I returned to the area around my hotel and found a modest place to eat dinner. I contemplated going out to experience more of the Parisienne nightlife but decided I would stay in and plan out my trip to Switzerland before going to bed.

Chapter 3

Zurich

Since the focus of my trip was France and Italy, I did not do a lot of research on Switzerland. My travel itinerary was extremely ambitious, given that I only had three weeks in total for the trip. Therefore, I decided I would visit just one Swiss city, Zurich, and I would have less than twenty-four hours to explore.

I took an early morning train from Paris to Zurich. Although there were faster trains, I went with a less expensive option, so the duration of the trip was a little longer, about six hours. I believe the pace of the trip was starting to catch up with me, so I slept a good part of the way.

By the time I arrived in Zurich, it was early afternoon. I knew I had a lot of ground to cover in a very short amount of time, so I went immediately to my hotel and checked in. I had booked an inexpensive but nice hotel in what is considered New Zurich. The check-in process was very efficient and professional, but the staff did not seem overly friendly. That was fine with me as I was in a hurry.

After I checked in, I dropped off my backpack in the room and immediately headed out to explore. The desk clerk gave me some directions on how to get to shopping and restaurants. I really had not eaten much, so my first order of business was to grab a quick lunch.

Venice Smile for Ellen

Knowing the Swiss are known for their watchmaking, I thought I would see if I could find one I could afford. My hotel was within walking distance of some of the shopping areas. I stopped in at several Swiss watch stores, but everything was out of my price range. Finally, I came upon a watch store that looked a little more reasonable and stepped in to browse. I was leaning over the glass displays when I was immediately greeted by a sharp-dressed, very attractive woman, "May I help you find something?" she said in English, with an accent. I told her I was looking for a watch, but I was on a limited budget. Her look was one of disappointment as she guided me over to a different section of the store. There, I spotted a silver Certina that was within striking distance of what I was willing to spend. I honestly was not much of a negotiator, but asked if that was the best they could do on the price.

She then produced a small calculator, punched in some numbers, and turned the display of the calculator around so I could see the final price. It looked like she took about 12% off, which I thought was quite reasonable. I was now the proud owner of my first Swiss watch. Out the door, I went wearing my new watch. I knew I had very little time to explore, but I would see what I could do. Using a street map I purchased at the train station, I was able to navigate my way to what is considered "Old Zurich". I must say, it was quite beautiful, and at that point, I wished I had allocated more time to Switzerland.

Old Zurich was clean and very easy to navigate. It has a sense of charm that made me feel comfortable. From what I could tell, most of the locals spoke German or at least a certain dialect of German.

It was early afternoon, and I was getting hungry so I decided I would find a nice place to stop in and enjoy lunch. I walked through the streets, looking at the menus of various restaurants, until I found something that sounded good. I found a place with a diverse menu, one where I could order a beer and a sandwich. The Swiss were extremely accommodating and quite efficient.

A nice young woman seated me immediately and within a few minutes, I was served my beer; and within ten minutes, my sandwich arrived. My table was at the back of the restaurant, small, made to seat two people. I had a good view of the restaurant, and while I was eating, I would occasionally glance around to see who else was in the restaurant. About fifteen feet away, I noticed a family of three sitting together, enjoying their lunch. It appeared to be a mother, father, and a young man, perhaps twenty years old. As I was enjoying my lunch, I noticed the young man started to choke on his food. I watched carefully, hoping he would naturally clear his air passage, but after a few seconds, it was obvious to me that his airway was completely blocked. The mother stood up in panic and started banging on her son's back. Nothing seemed to work, and the man was starting to turn blue. The father just sat there, almost indifferent to the whole incident.

I quickly stood up and ran to the table. By this time, the mother was yelling loudly in a language I did not recognize, assumingly asking the restaurant staff to call for help. I established eye contact with the mother and said, "I'm going to do the Heimlich maneuver. Are you ok with that"? She must have understood English as she shook her head in the affirmative and screamed loudly, "Yes!" I could not help but notice the father was still sitting in his chair, not expressing any emotion or concern.

After I graduated from college, I worked in a psychiatric hospital in Roanoke, Virginia. I graduated with a psychology and sociology degree and had hopes of becoming a psychologist. I moved from New York to Virginia in 1984 to do graduate work at Virginia Tech.

At the psychiatric center, I received training in the Heimlich maneuver and, in fact, executed it successfully twice on patients who were choking while eating in the cafeteria. The young man was now in full panic mode and began flailing his arms all around. While he was still sitting in his chair, I reached around his midsection just beneath his ribcage, clasped my hands together firmly, and pulled with all my strength on his abdomen, pulling him from a seated position to where I was holding him upright like a bear hug. The object, which turned out to be a chicken bone, immediately shot out of the man's mouth, ironically hitting his father in the chest. Within seconds, the man's face turned from panic to a huge smile. The mother started to pat me on the shoulder, smiling in gratitude. She was saying something to me, but I could not understand anything she was saying. The restaurant manager and a waiter came over and thanked me for intervening. The young man spoke a little English and said, "Thank you so much for helping me. Are you a doctor?"

I laughed aloud and said, "No, I'm a martial artist". I do not think he understood my humor, but offered his hand. I shook his hand and calmly returned to my table and finished my lunch. As I reflected on the incident, I became aggravated that the father never stood up to try to help his son or even offer any type of consolation. He also never even acknowledged my intervention.

In the very short time I had left, I managed to visit St. Peters Church, a very impressive historic structure with a huge clock face, perhaps one of the largest in all of Europe. I also took a picturesque ferry ride across Lake Zurich. Sadly, I didn't have much more time to experience all that Zurich had to offer because I wanted to make sure I had more time in Italy and Greece. I knew I would get back here again someday. I found my way back to my hotel and fell fast asleep, quite exhausted from walking all day.

Chapter 4

Venice

During the train ride from Zurich to Venice, I enjoyed the most beautiful scenery I had ever experienced. As the train cut through the mountains, I gazed out the windows for hours, totally impressed by the natural beauty of the land. Sitting directly across from me was a young family of four: husband, wife, a girl, and a boy, I guessed to be around seven years old. I was wearing a Club Med shirt (one that I purchased on the trip where I met Andrew). The husband pointed to my shirt and said something in a language I did not recognize. Turns out he was speaking Dutch. I said, "I'm sorry, I don't understand," then he said something in what I recognized to be German.

I said, "Oh, I don't speak German either".

He laughed and then said, "J'aime ta chemise," which is basic French for "I like your shirt." Turns out they were a Dutch family from somewhere in Belgium (I didn't recognize the city). They didn't speak English, and I didn't speak Dutch or German, but we both understood French enough to have a very pleasant conversation. I was quite impressed with how friendly they were and how curious they were about America. Talking to that young family really made my day, as I realized I have a passion for learning about different cultures, languages, and people.

The trip took about seven and a half hours, and I didn't sleep one minute. I enjoyed periodic chats with the family and took in the stunning views of the mountains.

By the time we pulled into Venice, it was already dark. Although certainly excited to be in Italy for the first time, I was starting to get tired. During my research, I discovered hotels were much cheaper if you stayed on the outskirts of what would be considered Venice proper. My plan was to get a cheap hotel, get some sleep, and head into Venice the next morning to explore the city fully. I walked around for about thirty minutes and stumbled upon a little hotel. I went in and was greeted by a nice woman at the front desk. Now, even though my heritage is Italian, I could not speak any Italian. Fortunately, the woman at the front desk could speak enough English to check me in and point me in the direction of my room. I quickly dropped off my backpack and headed out the door. My goal was to grab some dinner and head back to get some sleep.

I found a small little café and just ordered a turkey croissant and a beer; just trying to get something in my stomach. About this time, I was really starting to miss my boys. I found a pay phone and called my ex-wife's number. She picked up and sounded happy to hear from me.

After a few pleasant exchanges, she put the boys on the

phone one at a time. They were so cute and so sweet; I had tears running down my face. Our conversation was brief but very rewarding. After talking to Brett and Brandon, I was really feeling sad. I missed them so much and felt guilty being so far away from them for so long. I also started feeling a little sorry for myself. I had been in Europe for a week and really had not met anyone. I thought, *"What a dumbass for doing this trip by myself."* I felt like I was wasting it. "Wouldn't it be awesome to share this adventure with someone you were in a relationship with?" Next, I made another call this time, it was to my friend Andrew. He picked it up immediately, and it was great to hear his voice. I told him about my adventures exploring Amsterdam, Paris, and Zurich. I could tell he was genuinely excited that I was doing this trip.

However, Andrew was always good at reading people, and he could tell that something was wrong and said, "What's wrong….you are enjoying yourself, right?"

I said, "Yes, but honestly, I miss my kids, and I'm wondering if I made a mistake doing this trip by myself. I'm thinking of heading back to the States tomorrow".

Andrew's voice elevated significantly. I could feel his passion through the phone, and he said in his suave Canadian accent, "John, listen to me, you are NOT to cut your trip short. You need to finish out the remaining two weeks. Trust me. You will meet people.

You must see this through…no, no I won't let you".

At that point, I realized Andrew was right and snapped back, "Ok, ok….I get it…..I will stay".

After hanging up with Andrew, I headed back to the hotel. That night, I got a good night's sleep and felt rested in the morning. I was now ready to tackle Venice. I decided to leave my main backpack in a locker at the train station, as it was just too big and bulky to drag through Venice. I would have to come back and get it later. I grabbed a quick croissant and coffee and took a short train ride into Venice.

As soon as I got off the train and headed out to the platform, where all the boats departed for multiple city destinations, I was absolutely in awe. Venice, once a global power, is over 1200 years old, and many of the buildings I was looking at date back 800 years. The endless waterways connected over a hundred little islands formed in the Venetian Lagoon and were not like anything I had seen before. It was as if an ancient city suddenly emerged from the Adriatic Sea. As beautiful as Amsterdam was, Venice was unique in the way the city was organized.

Motorboats and gondolas were going in all different directions, people were buzzing about the city, and there was an uplifting energy. Instead of paved streets, countless waterways served as the major pathway for transit. Small boats replace buses, which taxi people from one part of the city to the next. Beautiful wooden powerboats usher people and supplies throughout the city. Gondolas of all shapes took couples from all over the world on romantic interludes.

It was September 6, and the temperature was reasonably warm. The sun was glistening off the canals, which gave the city the most gorgeous glow. I took a short boat taxi over to a popular docking station. I only knew it was popular by how many people got off at that stop.

My first view of the Grand Canal

I walked around the endless little alleyways, popped in and out of the shops, and occasionally stopped to rest and people-watch. By afternoon, it was getting a little warm. I noticed my hair was getting long and was rather uncomfortable. I stumbled upon an old-fashioned barbershop and figured, "What the hell— I might as well experience the culture."

I walked in and was welcomed by a short little man standing by an empty barber chair. With a smile and a "Buongiorno," he gestured to me to have a seat in the barber chair and introduced himself as Francesco.

As I looked around the room, I noticed six older Italian men sitting around talking and reading magazines. It took me a few minutes to realize they were not there for haircuts. This was their hangout, where they met with friends and socialize. Francesco was very nice and spoke good English with a charming accent. He asked all about my journey and listened intently. I could tell from our short time together that he was a good man, a third-generation barber who had lived his entire life in Venice.

After about twenty minutes, he was done. When I went to pay him, I gave him extra in the form of a tip. At this point, I was going to learn a life lesson. The man looked at me with a smile and said, "You Americans….you pay more than the service demands……not necessary". I realized that it was almost an insult. Someone later explained to me that the Europeans sometimes see tipping as we are offering them charity, and hardworking, proud Europeans do not need our charity. "Ah, I get it."

St. Mark's Square

After my haircut, I was feeling refreshed and figured it was time for more exploring. I found my way over to St. Mark's Square, or Piazza San Marco as it is officially named, to see the famous Basilica.

When I first entered the square, I was completely amazed as I walked all around. It was bigger than I had imagined: a massive open-air plaza where ancient buildings formed the shape of a square. Hundreds of pigeons were flying around my head and bopping around the ancient stone ground, looking for scraps of food. I had read in my travel books that the original version of the square was built in the 9th century and then expanded over the centuries. I'm not an architecture expert by any means, but I knew enough to understand I was seeing something quite exceptional.

The buildings were all a little different, yet complimented each other nicely. I would later learn that some of the buildings represented Byzantine architecture, and some were Gothic. There was an impressive 500-year-old clock tower, and a long arcade-type set of buildings (Procuratie Vecchie) with cafes, art galleries, and retail stores. People from all over the world were buzzing around, snapping pictures, and—sitting in outdoor cafes, enjoying the stunning centuries-old gathering place over a cup of coffee or a glass of wine. St. Mark's Basilica is so grand that it naturally stands out as the focal point of the square. Its decorative arches, domes, and steeples jetting into the sky were so impressive I had to just stand there for a minute to fully absorb its charm. I was astonished by this massive structure, which was originally built between c829-c836; it has been rebuilt over the years. The actual structure I saw opened in 1094. I was moved by what I was looking at! It was like something out of a movie.

As I entered the Basilica and looked around inside, I became emotional and teared up. The floors, walls, statues, and windows were all so beautiful and ornately decorated. It was grandiose yet intimate, warm, and inviting. The paintings on the walls, arches, and ceiling told countless biblical stories. It was as if, somehow, I had been transported into the bible itself and was getting a chance to walk through the ages. After about an hour, I decided to move on and find out what else I could see. I exited the Basilica and randomly picked one of the many walkway options as my next destination.

Ellen

The sun was high in the sky. It was getting hot but still comfortable. As I was meandering through all the little sidewalks and enjoying the scenery, I turned the corner of one of the many Venice side streets. I looked over my left shoulder, and standing there in front of a store about twenty-five feet away was a beautiful young woman. She was slender, had medium-length brown hair, and was wearing a skirt showing her very pretty legs. I would say she was in her early 30s, petite, in shape, and obviously athletic– just my type. I was not sure if she was an American or European. She obviously saw me almost trip over myself and stare at her, and she smiled. And it was a smile that lit up the entire square; and at that moment, it was as if the city of Venice came alive.

I stopped suddenly and quite deliberately and turned around, almost now completely facing her. I did not want to be ridiculously obvious, as I did not know if she was with someone. I noticed a very handsome man standing next to her, but was not sure if they were together. Knowing my luck, she is with that Italian dude. I needed a stall tactic to assess the opportunities, so I reached into my backpack, pulled out a map, and started looking at it as if I was lost and trying to find my way.

She must have known I was checking her out; as a couple of moments later, while I was pretending to look at my street map, she started walking towards me. I started to panic, "Uh oh, she is coming towards me….now what"…..what am I going to say?" She walked very deliberately and with such confidence.

She came right up to me, and before I could open my mouth, she said, "Hello." I think my mouth was open, and I was still fumbling with the blasted map. I managed to pull together a smile and said, "Hi."

"Why are you looking at a map of Paris – you do know you're in Venice –right?" she said very sarcastically.

I looked down at my map, and sure enough, in bold red letters was "Paris." I was busted. As soon as she began to speak, I could tell by her accent she was from New York. Now, not the New York I was from (Western New York). I figured she was from the other New York…New York City. I did not exactly know what to say and was admittedly a little nervous. After all, except for a couple of pleasantries with the young woman at the Arc de Triumph, I had not talked to any women, not any that I might be romantically interested in anyway.

I said, "I take it you are from New York City."

She smiled and said, "Good guess, I'm from Long Island originally, but I live in San Diego now."

Feeling a little more comfortable that we had broken the ice, I responded, "I live in Chicago now, but I'm from Western New York originally, a small town south of Buffalo."

I was getting "I'm John" out of my mouth when another young woman walked over to us. It seems she was traveling with two other girls on a little European get-away and was currently shopping for lace, one of the products for which Venice is famous. About that time, my new friend introduced herself as Ellen. Her friend's name was Judy, and I could tell just by the way she talked that she was a real sweet person… nice big smile and lots of energy. She genuinely seemed happy to meet me. The other friend then joined us. Her name was Cynthia, and very pleasant, but seemingly disinterested, Ellen was talking to me.

After just a few minutes, Cynthia said to the girls, "Shall we go?" I thought, "Well, that was short-lived. She's going to get pulled away by her friends, and that will be that".

Just as I was ready to open my mouth and blurt out, "Well, it was nice meeting you. Enjoy your vacation" (how lame is that), Ellen said, "You know, we are just heading over to St. Marks to tour the cathedral if you would like to come along."

I could hear my internal voice say, "Now, why didn't I think of that?" Not caring that I had just spent an hour exploring St. Marks just a few minutes earlier, I responded, "I have always wanted to see St. Marks," and off we went. It did not take long to get to St. Mark's from where I had met the girls. Cynthia and Judy were kind enough to give Ellen and me a little time to talk as they kept a little bit of distance between us. I also noticed that somewhere along the walk to St. Mark's the guy that was standing next to Ellen when I first spotted her had joined us. I later found out that he was hanging around with Cynthia.

We walked into St. Mark's and still did not own up to Ellen that I had already seen it. It was fine because, for me, it was just as beautiful the second time through it. Raised Catholic, I was always very respectful in churches, especially ones as well-known and prestigious as St. Marks. The cathedral was full of visitors praying at the Stations of the Cross. While we were walking through, I was whispering quietly and walking very gingerly through the various points of interest. Ellen was talking and did not seem quite as into seeing the entire beautiful decorative interior as I was.

After just a very few minutes, I could see Ellen was making her way toward the exit; she had apparently seen enough. I thought, "Well, that didn't take long."   After we exited St. Mark's, I was not sure where we were going next, or for that matter, if I was even invited. However, I decided I was just going with the flow. No one really seemed to have a plan, and we all just walked as a group through beautiful St. Mark's Square. Everyone continued to give Ellen and me some space. I was not sure if that was by design–perhaps Ellen said something to the girls. More likely, they had just read the signals and decided to give us some time to talk, which I appreciated.

During our stroll through the square and then onto the many little streets of Venice, we walked in and out of countless little shops. We found our way over to the famous Rialto Bridge, a four-hundred-year-old bridge connecting the districts of San Marco and San Polo. We decided to stop at a café near the foot of the bridge to enjoy a cup of coffee and talk while Cynthia and Judy were off shopping.

During that period, Ellen and I had time to get to know each other a little bit. We quickly discovered that we both went to State University of New York (SUNY) schools. I attended Geneseo State, and she attended Oswego State. Although Ellen never revealed her age, I had figured we were close in age, although she was likely a few years younger.

Ellen had never been married and did not seem to have a boyfriend back home waiting for her. I told her I was divorced but did not offer that I had two little boys back home. I thought it was a little early to be springing that on her. Ellen was very inquisitive and seemed to have a genuine and caring disposition. I could tell she was a great conversationalist. She asked good questions and responded to questions well, and I honestly enjoyed talking with her. It did not take long for me to figure out that this young woman had a unique passion and zest for life. I was immediately attracted to her confidence and energy level, and it was obvious she was quite intelligent. As we walked along further, we each shared some of our dating experiences, taking the opportunity to poke at some of the disappointments, failures, and, in some cases, disasters. It came out that some years back, Ellen had been in a very serious relationship, and in fact, they had apparently been discussing marriage. I did not find out what happened, but I assume he broke up with her as the wounds were still very fresh, and I could tell Ellen had been hurt. Somewhere along the way, the topic of kids came up, and Ellen said, "Oh, I could never date a guy with kids."

I just smiled and said, "Oh, I don't know, you might not want to limit yourself as such." She did not probe any further, and I still did not feel comfortable telling her I had children, at least not yet.

After soaking in the beauty of the Rialto Bridge, Ellen and I continued our walk through the streets of Venice. The conversation between the two of us was quite natural. Ellen always spoke with such enthusiasm. Her zest for life was like a magnet for me, and I was excited to have the opportunity to get to know her more. We came upon one of the beautiful canals where you could take a ride on a gondola. Well, I was thinking while in Venice, you absolutely must do the gondola thing. I looked at Ellen and said, "What do you think?"

She responded quite energetically, "Sure, sounds fun."

I started walking away quickly, and Ellen said, "Where are you going?"

I looked back with a smile and said, "I will be right back."

I literally ran down the street to a café we had walked by earlier. I ran into the shop in a hurry, ordered a bottle of wine, and asked the nice man if he had two wine glasses I could also buy. He would not be able to sell me wine glasses, but he did manage to produce plastic cups, which I would just have to do. After all, I was in a hurry. I exited quickly and went sprinting down the street to where Ellen was standing. I did not think I was gone long, but Ellen seemed rather concerned.

As I raised the bottle of wine so Ellen could see it, I said, "Now we can go."

Ellen's gave me that wonderful smile and said, "That was sweet. Hey, the girls are going with us".

The sun was just beginning to set, so it seemed like the perfect time for our little romantic gondola ride. In the little inlet, there were quite a few gondolier options. Until this moment, the only experience I had with gondola rides was from what I saw in movies or travel books. From my research, I recall that quite often, the career of the gondolier is passed on from generation to generation; Venice limits the number of gondola operators. To select the gondolier for Ellen and me, I just looked around and saw a man standing in is gondola with a big smile, and he seemed to wave us over. We quickly walked over to greet the man, and I helped Ellen and the girls get into the gondola. I quickly followed, making sure not to drop my bottle of wine.

The gondolier introduced himself as Domenico. I guessed he was in his early fifties, with grey hair, handsome, wearing a white button-down shirt and black slacks. He quickly launched his boat and started down one of the little canals that went in multiple directions. I had recalled from the movies that some gondoliers sing for you. Although Domenico did not sing, he was very nice; and in broken English, he gave us a nice tour of the Venice canals, describing all the buildings and some of the history. While we were weaving in and out of the various canals, I poured us a nice glass of wine and just took in the pure beauty of the Venice evening.

All the buildings lit up beautifully in sync with the setting sun. It was quite romantic. I was thinking, "Yesterday, I was depressed, feeling sorry for myself, and ready to leave for home. Today, I'm sipping wine on a gondola touring the canals of Venice with a beautiful woman".

"Thank you, Andrew!"

Ellen was now starting to warm up to me a little and scooted closer to me. Taking into consideration the amazing atmosphere and romantic setting, Ellen looked quite beautiful sitting there. I could not resist any longer, so I gently put my hand on her knee. I was testing the waters a little to see how receptive she would be. Happily,

Ellen didn't toss me overboard. Just about this time, our gondolier was trying to get our attention and pointed to a man in the distance who had opened the window of one of the buildings on the canal. The man had a huge, welcoming smile, and as we pulled up, he leaned out of the window further with a bottle of wine and filled our cups.

Our gondolier and the man exchanged a few words in Italian and off we went again down the canal. Ellen said, "Now that was pretty awesome." Ellen and I just smiled at each other. It doesn't get much better than this. For the rest of our ride, we spent more time getting to know each other. Conversations flowed very easily, and before we knew it, our gondolier was starting to navigate us back into the docking area.

Ellen and John on the Gondola – Day 1

I have never had a good sense of direction, and honestly, Venice was quite a challenge for me. Being the man, I figured I should at least look like I knew what I was doing, so I said to Ellen, "OK, should we head back to St. Mark's Square and find something to eat and drink?" and I selected one of the many little pathways and started walking.

Ellen quickly yelled out, "You are going the wrong way, it's this way," as she pointed in the opposite direction. It turns out she was right. I quickly discovered that Ellen had an amazing internal compass and always seemed to know where she was going. I recalled asking her if she had spent a lot of time in Venice. Turns out that it was her very first time visiting Venice as well. I figured, "Ah, what the hell, I'll just follow her lead."

As we were getting closer to St. Mark's Square, we came upon a street artist who was sitting there painting his next masterpiece. The artist's name was Marco, and he had a small little wall behind him where he displayed his artwork. All his work was of Venice images, landscapes, canals, bridges, and buildings, and his work was quite impressive.

Ellen said to me, "Should I get one to remember my time in Venice?" I said, "Sure, I think that would be great." Ellen picked out a very small painting of a gondola-style long boat sitting on a canal with centuries-old buildings in the background. We said goodbye to Marco, and off we went.

The painting Ellen bought from Marco in Venice

By this time, everyone was getting hungry, so we started to look for a nice place to grab dinner. After weaving through a few more alleys, we came upon a quaint little restaurant with outdoor seating. We secured a table large enough for all of us and sat down to relax.

I believe everyone was tired from a long day of exploration and shopping. A waiter immediately appeared from the inside of the restaurant with a big smile and a pleasant greeting. Someone must have quickly ordered wine because it seemed like only seconds passed before another waiter came out with a huge jug of red wine. You must know that until this trip, I was a beer drinker.

I never drank wine at all, so this was an entirely new experience. I had just shared a bottle of wine with Ellen on the gondola, and truthfully, I probably drank 2/3 of it. I thought, "-When in Rome… or in this case, Venice, I will drink wine with dinner like everyone else."

Soon after, a huge basket of bread materialized. We all ordered individual pasta dishes, and as we were eating more wine was delivered to the table. I did not realize this at the time, but as most of our party was appropriately pacing themselves, I was drinking the wine like water. Our dinner lasted a couple of hours as we were all talking, people-watching, and enjoying the beautiful Venice evening.

Ellen and I continued to get to know each other, and it seemed like things between us were developing nicely. After a while, we agreed that we were all tired. The girls were ready to head back to their hotel. I had almost forgotten that my hotel was an exceptionally long distance away as I was travelling cheaply and tried to save money by picking a hotel outside of Venice.

We paid our bill, said goodbye to our wonderful waiter, and we all stood up to go. As I stood up, the gallons of wine I drank hit me like a ton of bricks. I quickly realized that I was quite intoxicated. Although I thought I was standing still, Ellen noticed I was swaying back and forth, unable to keep my balance. As we began to walk, I could barely keep a straight line. Trying to help, Ellen put her arm around me, attempting to prop me up, which was difficult to do as she was all of 110lbs, and I weighed 175lbs.

This went on for a while and I could tell Ellen was less than happy that I allowed myself to get sloshed. However, she at least liked me enough to attempt to help. As we were walking and talking, she said, "John, I don't think you are going to be able to make it back to your hotel by yourself." Since I was not in the right state of mind, I said, "Oh, no problem, I'll be ok. You don't need to worry about me."

By this time, we had arrived at the hotel where Ellen was staying. Judy and Cynthia said good night and went into the hotel, while Ellen stayed out front with me. I attempted to say good night to Ellen and told her I would come back and see her in the morning. As I attempted to walk away, Ellen noticed I was still in no condition to try to navigate my way back out of Venice via boat and train.

She said, "John, I have an idea; it's late. You should just stay in our hotel tonight. You can sleep on the floor in our room. I am sure the girls will not mind." At this point, I realized Ellen was most likely right, so I agreed. We walked into the hotel lobby. It was obvious I was still unsteady on my feet, and as Ellen was trying to guide me up the stairs to her hotel room, the hotel manager quickly appeared and asked what we were doing. Ellen explained the situation and the manager said since I was not a registered guest, I would not be able to stay in the hotel.

Ellen then attempted to explain that I was her fiancé and it would be fine. The manager more insistently said in a very heavy Italian accent, "Not possible." After Ellen tried several more times to convince the manager, he was not giving in. I then said, "Well, I will just pay for my own room then."

Well, it was obvious the manager did not want any drunken fool staying in his hotel as he quickly stated, "We have no availability."

Ellen, being extremely sharp and fast thinking, quickly guided me back out to the front of the hotel and said, "Don't worry, we will go find you another hotel nearby to stay."

Off we went with Ellen still propping me up. We probably visited four more hotels over the next hour, and all of them said they were at capacity. By this time, I could tell Ellen was exhausted and quite frustrated with the whole situation. We stopped in the middle of an old square, and Ellen looked sternly at me and said, "John, I'm sorry, but I'm tired, and I just want to go back to my hotel and go to sleep. I think you are on your own now."

I quickly responded, "That's fine, of course, I will be just fine." I totally understood; after all, it was quite late, and we were both very tired. I walked with Ellen back to her hotel. There was no kiss, no hug, and I knew she was exhausted and upset with me.

She said good night, and I saw her disappear through the hotel's front door. I did not even have her number or contact information. I was wondering how I would ever see her again. However, at this moment, I had to focus on something more pressing: my survival. I just started walking back through the maze of streets.

Venice is a very beautiful city, but it's also a very complicated city full of countless little bridges, corridors, canals, and buildings. My sense of direction was poor when I was stone-cold sober, let alone when I was ploughed on cheap red wine. I wandered aimlessly for what seemed like another hour and a half.

No restaurants or stores were open, the streets were dark, and I was quite lost. I tried to stop in at two more hotels, but to my surprise, none of their doors were open, and no one would come to the door. I thought to myself, "Well, this is crazy. In the good ole USA, the hotels are open 24 hours." I continued to stumble down through the corridors, and I noticed I was finally starting to sober up a bit.

The streets were completely empty, but I noticed in the distance crowds of people were all heading in the same direction. I was thinking wherever they are going, there must be life, possibly even a hotel that is open. I quickly caught up to the crowd and joined them as if I was a local. I figured out that they were heading to a boat docking station.

As we arrived at the dock, within minutes, a boat taxi pulled up, and we all got in. Mind you, I had no idea where that taxi was going, and honestly, at this point, I did not care. I was exhausted, had a nasty headache, and had to find a restroom.

That taxi must have gone fifteen or twenty minutes, which seemed like a lifetime to me. We finally arrived at the dock, and everyone got off. All the locals went in different directions, heading home, I supposed. I glanced up the street and saw a hotel that seemed to be still open. I quickly made a beeline for the hotel and as I approached the front door, I was almost praying that the door was still unlocked.

I reached out and grabbed the doorknob, and sure enough, it opened. I walked in quickly and found a nice man standing behind the counter. I said, "Can I get a room for the night?" He said, "But of course, sir." I did not ask any questions. I did not know how much the room cost, and I did not care. I was exhausted and just wanted to sleep. The man grabbed the key to the room and asked me to follow him. He took me outside of the hotel and guided me down the street to a different building, yet another new experience for me.

The manager opened the door to the building and pointed down to the hall where my room was. He gave me a key card and said good night. I opened the door and walked in. The room was pitch dark, and try as I might, in my drunken stupor, I could not figure out how to turn on the lights. I found out later I was supposed to insert that key card into a slot on the wall that would activate the electricity. At this point, I did not care about the lights. I found the bathroom and frantically relieved myself. By feeling my way around, I found what seemed like the shape of a bed, fell into it and passed out.

When I woke up, I noticed the sun beaming through these two huge bay windows, and I had to squint a bit to see. As I opened my eyes further, I was finally able to get a look at the room I booked, something I could not see the night before because I was too intoxicated to figure out how to turn on the lights. Suddenly, a feeling of shock came over me.

The room had palatial marble floors, ornate furniture, and beautiful artwork on the walls. During my entire trip, I was staying in modest hotels to keep costs down; now, I was seemingly in five-star accommodations. In all my life, I had not stayed in a hotel as nice as this one. I could not imagine what this was going to cost. I would have to deal with that later as I had bigger priorities.

Although I probably only slept five hours, it was morning, the sun was up, and I recalled Ellen and her friends were leaving Venice this morning. I thought to myself, "I must get back to her hotel and see her again." I figured I would at least get her contact information so I could get in touch with her when we were back in the United States. I was very hung over with a pounding headache; my eyes were burning, and I did not get enough sleep. However, I was determined to take a quick shower, check out, and see if I could find Ellen's hotel.

I found my way to the bathroom and again was in shock. The bathroom was huge, all marble tile, top of the line fixtures, and a huge shower. While showering, I said outloud, "I could park my car in here, it's so big." I took a shower but did not have a razor to shave. That was fine, as I did not have much time anyway. Since my backpack was in a locker somewhere on the other side of Venice, I had to put the same clothes back on that I had worn the night before.

As quickly as I could, I exited the building where my room was. Fortunately, I at least remembered the hotel lobby was about seventy-five feet down the street. I rushed towards the lobby and went in. A very nice man with a huge smile greeted me, but I was in no mood for pleasantries. "Checking out," I said rather insistently. While I was afraid to see the bill for a room I was in for less than six hours, I tried to put it out of my mind.

The clerk handed me the invoice, and sure enough, the cost was twenty times what I had been paying for the entire trip. I rolled my eyes, got out my credit card, and paid the man. Out the door, I went making my way back to the dock I had departed from the night before. While I did not exactly remember much about how I got from Ellen's hotel to my current location, I at least did remember which direction the boat was going when I was dropped off. I waited for the appropriate boat to go in the opposite direction and quickly boarded.

The next challenge was to figure out which dock I needed to exit. Since it was pitch dark last night, I had no landmarks to go by, so I decided to go by approximate time. After about fifteen minutes, we came upon a dock that looked familiar, so I figured I would try this exit. By this time, I was starting to panic because I remembered Ellen saying they were checking out early. The boat was packed, and I was doing my best to get off the boat quickly as soon as it docked.

I must have cut in front of this old woman because she literally grabbed my shoulder and pushed me aside. I am quite certain she cursed at me in Italian as it sounded a lot like when my grandmother would curse in Italian at the TV set every time, she watched soap operas. I humbled myself and waited my turn in line.

As soon as one of the stewards let us exit, I quickly started walking up the street. Now, I was completely lost. All the little alleyways looked the same to me, and I had no idea in which direction Ellen's hotel was located. I was getting upset with myself, as I did not even have the name of the hotel. If I had that, I could ask someone where it was.

After about fifteen minutes of frantically weaving my way through the various little corridors, I stumbled upon the square where Ellen bought her painting.

Sure enough, there was Marco at his station painting away. I know this may sound crazy, but I was so happy to see Marco that I literally went running up to him and shouted, "Marco!" as if we were old friends. He had this blank look on his face, and I could tell that he did not remember me. I said, "Marco, hi, listen, I was here yesterday with my friend, and we bought a painting from you. I'm trying to find the hotel she is staying in."

He just smiled at me and said, "Si." Though I could not remember the name of the hotel, I was able to remember what it looked like. After all, the hotel manager practically threw me out the front door, so I did remember some information about the hotel. I described the hotel to Marco, and he nodded in the affirmative and pointed down the street. I slapped him on the back, thanked him, and started jogging in the direction where Marco pointed.

After just a few minutes, sure enough, I came upon Ellen's hotel. I was so relieved. I surprised myself that I was able to find my way back to the hotel after the night I had. I jogged up to the courtyard in front of the hotel. As I was planning to enter the lobby, Ellen's friend Judy came out of the front door. Judy quickly spotted me and had this confused look on her face.

She said, "John, what are you doing back here? I thought you were leaving."

I said, "Judy, hi, yes, I did leave, but now I'm back. I want to see Ellen again before you all leave. Is Ellen in her room?"

Judy smiled warmly and said, "Yes, Ellen and Cynthia are in the room. I was just heading out to find some coffee. You wait here, and I will go tell Ellen you are out here." Like a desperate child, I responded, "Thank you so much, Judy. I really appreciate that. I'll just be right here." About this time, fatigue was starting to catch up with me, so I found a bench and sat down.

A few minutes later, Judy came back out and said, "I told Ellen you were here. She is getting dressed. She will be down a bit." Judy then disappeared down the street looking for coffee. I literally closed my eyes as they were burning, and I was just not feeling very well. About fifteen minutes later, Judy came back through with coffee. She asked, "Ellen still hasn't come down?" Rather irritated, I responded, "Not yet." Judy then walked into the hotel lobby. Another forty-five minutes passed, and Ellen still had not come down.

I was now getting aggravated. I was trying to think why she would not want to see me. I know she was not happy with me getting drunk on cheap wine, but I thought we had a great day together overall; and thought we were developing a connection. I did not yet have a chance to get breakfast or even a cup of coffee for that matter. I was hungry and still hung over. All my belongings were in a locker somewhere, and I was not even sure if I could find them again. I thought, I would give her a few more minutes. If she does not come down, she doesn't want to see me. I will just get on my way and head to Rome, which was my next intended destination.

Just as I stood up to leave, I saw Ellen appear in the doorway of the hotel. The sun caught her just right, and she was even more beautiful than I had remembered. While I was a haggard wreck, unshaven, and wearing dirty clothes, she was freshly showered and looked like she had a good night's sleep. Once again, she gave me that great smile, and I practically melted. I was so happy that I was able to see her again.

Ellen walked down the steps towards me and said, "Judy told me you were out here. What are you doing?" I responded, "Yes, I have been out here waiting for you for over an hour. I was thinking you did not want to see me, so I was getting ready to leave." Ellen did not apologize but simply said, "I just woke up; I needed my coffee and a shower." I was not sure if I should be angrier by her explanation or relieved. I said, "That's ok. I realized that with everything going on last night, we did not exchange contact information, and I was afraid I would not be able to contact you again."

Ellen smiled and said, "Well, it's good that you came back then, isn't it? Where did you end up staying last night?" With a heavy sigh, I said, "That will have to be a story for another time." Ellen laughed and said, "OK, well, listen, we are heading to Bologna today. I think you were planning to go directly to Rome, but if you would like to go to Bologna with us, we are planning to head to Rome sometime tomorrow." I said, "Yes, that would be great. I can serve as your bodyguard and luggage handler. The problem is I haven't had a chance to retrieve my backpack from the locker I left it in; as you can see, I'm still wearing the same clothes I had on last night, but I did at least take a shower."

Ellen was so quick in her thinking and said, "What about this? There are some shops very close to here, let's go and at least get you a fresh shirt to wear. Then I will finish packing while you go find your backpack. We will meet you at the train station in a couple of hours, and we will all go to Bologna together. I thought that was a great plan and said, "That sounds good to me."

Ellen started to walk towards one of the small corridors as if she knew exactly where she was going, with me close behind. It seemed like it took maybe five minutes or so and we came upon what looked like a men's clothing store. We went in, and since we knew we did not have a lot of time, Ellen went right to the store clerk and told him what we were looking for. The nice man took us over to one of the tables where an assortment of men's shirts was on display.

Ellen looked through the shirts and picked up a red, short-sleeved shirt. It looked two sizes small, very European, and nothing like what I would pick for myself. I said to Ellen, "Really?" She said, "Yes, trust me." I purchased the shirt, went into the changing room, and put it on. When I came out, Ellen tilted her head, looked at me, and said, "That will do nicely." Out the door we went.

While we were walking back to Ellen's hotel, we came upon one of those beautiful bridges that connect the islands. Ellen stopped me and said, "Let's get a picture of us on this bridge." Ellen was much more forward than me and flagged down some poor local woman, probably trying to get to work or something. "Would you mind taking a picture of us, please?" she asked. The woman stopped and was quite accommodating. She nodded in the affirmative and said, "Si," as Ellen handed her the camera.

Ellen and I positioned ourselves on the bridge, and to my surprise, she put both of her arms around my waist. I responded by putting my arm around her shoulder. It seemed quite natural, which seemed odd to me since we had just met the day before. We then walked quickly back to the hotel; I was sure Cynthia and Judy would be waiting for Ellen. Ellen started walking towards the hotel door, looked back, and said, "OK, we will see you at the train station in a couple of hours." As she entered the hotel, I sighed heavily as I realized, "I did it again. I did not get her phone number or email. I'm a complete idiot."

Ellen and John on the bridge - Day 2
Notice, wearing the watch just purchased in
Zurich

At this point, all I could do was hope she would be at the train station as planned. I considered going into the hotel to see if I could get her information; then the thought of another confrontation with that hotel manager made me think otherwise. By this time, I was starting to wake up a little, and a plan to find my backpack started to formulate in my mind. I knew if I got back to the Grand Canal, I could take a boat taxi to the general location where I left my backpack in the locker. I had a general idea of where the Grand Canal was and started heading in that direction. After about ten minutes, I came upon one of the docks and just started asking the men on the dock where I could get a taxi to the train station.

After a few minutes, I found a nice taxi man who said he could take me. His boat was quite beautiful, an older wooden boat that was in great shape. As we sped off down the canal, the sunlight was reflecting off the water, and I was finally able to sit back and enjoy the immense beauty of Venice. Although tired, I was feeling energized by thinking of my last twenty-four hours. I did not know where this thing with Ellen was going. All I knew was that I wanted to see her again. A big smile came upon my face.

The ride over to the train station did not seem to take that long. I paid the nice man, jumped out of the boat, and watched him speed off down the canal. Once back at the train station, everything began to look familiar to me, and I knew exactly where the bank of lockers was where I left my main backpack.

After retrieving my backpack, I realized I now had some time to get some much-needed coffee and breakfast. I found a nice little place in the station serving breakfast. I was so hungry by this time and woofed down a coffee and two croissants.

I still had some time before the girls showed up, so I decided to check the train schedules. Since my original plan was to go directly to Rome, I had not done any research on Bologna. I was able to find out there were plenty of train options. We would be travelling southwest, and it would take a little over two hours to get there. I plopped myself down on a bench in the middle of the station so I could see the girls when they arrived.

I then started to wonder what I would do if they did not show up. Maybe Ellen really did not want me tagging along with them any longer, and they were going to do something else today. They could easily ditch me, but I figured I really had no choice but to wait and see what happened. About thirty minutes later, sure enough, the girls arrived with their suitcases in tow. They looked rested and in good spirits.

Despite all my worrying, I could tell Ellen was sincerely happy to see me. As she walked up to me, she smiled and said, "So you found your backpack? That is a big backpack. How do you carry that thing?" A huge feeling of joy poured over me.

Chapter 5

Bologna

The ride to Bologna was uneventful. Ellen and I sat next to each other, and we talked a little, but she knew I was exhausted and did not seem to mind when I closed my eyes to take a little nap. When I woke up and opened my eyes, I could see Ellen was watching me. She smiled and said, "We are pulling into Bologna." Ellen and the girls decided we should check into a hotel first and drop off our stuff; then, we could make time to explore.

It was exciting pulling into a different European city by train. After we collected our things and exited the train, we went into the main station to decide how we would get to the hotel. We discovered the train station was on the northern edge of the city center. I am not sure who picked the hotel, but I know it was not me. Anyway, one of the girls had selected a nice little hotel near the Piazza Maggiore, one of Bologna's largest and most important squares.

Since the hotel was within walking distance, we decided we would ignore the countless taxi drivers trying to get our attention. Well, that turned out not to be the best decision. While I was in good shape with a backpack, the girls had to drag their big luggage through about eight city blocks.

I tried to help where I could, but it was a comedy scene. We eventually found the hotel and walked into the lobby, a bit frustrated and overheated. By American standards, the hotel was probably 3.5 stars, small, quaint, and very European. After what happened in Venice, I was totally fine with staying in modest accommodations.

We quickly checked in and made plans to meet back down in the lobby in about an hour. While the girls were getting ready, I was able to do a little research. Although Bologna was not among my original target places to visit, I was excited that meeting Ellen allowed me to experience another great city. I had allowed some flexibility in my travel plans for just such an occasion. That is one of the reasons I did not spend a lot of time in Zurich, as I really wanted more time in Italy and Greece for my first trip to Europe.

My thought was that at some point in my life, I would get back to Switzerland and spend more time there. Bologna is a northern medieval city in the central portion of the country, with the Adriatic Sea to the east and the Tyrrhenian Sea to the west. Like many Italian cities, Bologna has its own rich identity and charm. It is a small city compared to Venice or Rome, with only about fifty-four square miles and a population of 388,000. The size and layout of Bologna was perfect to explore on foot.

I was so excited so I headed down to the lobby a little early and just sat there watching people come and go. The girls joined soon after and we planned to walk through the Piazza Maggiore as that seemed to be a central focus point in Bologna. As we started walking, I was impressed by Bologna and was wondering why visiting this medieval little town was not initially on my radar. Countless little outdoor cafes lined the city, with locals seemingly enjoying some good food and a lunchtime glass of wine. Ellen later told me that Bologna was known for its amazing food. There did not seem to be as many tourists as Venice, which made it even more appealing.

As we were walking through the streets of Bologna, we came upon a huge market. I had never seen anything quite like it. There were seemingly hundreds of merchants set up in unique little booths selling everything from leather to jewellery, clothes, and souvenirs. I think we spent over an hour there. I knew from our time together in Venice that Ellen loved to browse and shop. She really enjoyed walking through the market, although I do not think any of us bought anything, which was fine as we had a great time.

We eventually found our way to Piazza Maggiore, and it seemed like we had stepped through a time portal as the buildings looked very much like they did in the 15th century. We stopped by the beautiful Fountain of Neptune, a grand fountain and statue of the god Neptune, built in 1566. It was quite amazing to me that this fountain had been a gathering place for many Italians almost 200 years before the United States existed.

Although we did not go in, we walked by the impressive University of Bologna, which I would later learn is the world's oldest university in continuous operation, founded in 1088. It has also earned a reputation over the years as being one of the most beautiful universities in the world based on its stunning architecture, botanical gardens, and landscape. With the university being such a focal point of the city, Bologna had a high population of young students.

In the 12th and 13th centuries, Bologna was considered a city of grand towers. In those days, the wealthiest of families would build towers for defense purposes. Over the centuries, time took its toll on many of the towers, now either demolished or collapsed on their own. Not too far from Piazza Maggiore, we visited two of Bologna's famous remaining towers, the Asinelli Tower and the Tower of Garisenda.

Memorable for me was visiting Basilica Petronio, one of the largest churches in the world. The 14th-century basilica is a focal point in Piazza Maggiore, and for good ole Catholic boys like me, it was stunning to see. Other spectacular points of interest that we observed walking around Bologna included palaces, museums, and a gorgeous century-old library.

After touring the city, we all took a taxi to a local restaurant that our hotel desk manager recommended. As we pulled up to the restaurant, I could see crowds of people standing right out in front, so I figured this was going to be a fun place. I told the girls to go ahead and I would pay the driver. As I got out of the taxi, I noticed a few local Italian young men had already swarmed the girls. I laughed to myself as it only took me a minute to pay the taxi driver, and already, the local men were hitting on the girls.

I got the feeling that the local men did this a lot – waited around waiting for young women tourists to come by. I quickly went up to Ellen and put my hand on her shoulder as if to make it known she was with me. Of course, Ellen and I really were not together romantically, but I remained hopeful, and I was not going to let these young Italian studs interfere. I might have been more perturbed if the young Italians had not been so charming. I quickly surmised they were just fun-loving young men looking to have a good time.

Together, we all went into the restaurant, which was more of a bar that also served food. It was a quaint place but was bigger inside than it looked from the outside. There was a long bar on the left with several bar tenders serving drinks to a full bar of thirsty patrons, many of whom I assume were locals. To the right of the bar was a huge area, which looked like it served as a place to eat and perhaps a dance floor at night.

As soon as we walked in, a waiter immediately appeared and took our drink orders. The music was playing loudly, and the atmosphere was fun and lively. The waiter asked where we were from and as soon as we told him we were from the United States, he shouted over to the bartenders something in Italian. I assume he told him we were Americans. Next thing I knew, one of the bartenders headed over to the front door of the restaurant and closed the doors. Someone turned up the music, and the party got started.

As we were enjoying our drinks, Dean Martin's "Amore" started playing. The tables that were in the middle of the floor were quickly moved off to the side and it seemed like everyone in the bar got up and started dancing. It was an amazing experience. Ellen and I looked at each other almost at the same time, grabbed each other, and began to slow-dance. With the music blaring, everyone singing, "That's Amore." With Ellen finally in my arms, the stage was now set for me to make my first move.

I leaned in for a kiss and I was happy that Ellen was receptive. We did not kiss long, but it was long enough for both of us to realize that something special was happening. We ended up spending a couple of hours in that little bar, and we all had so much fun. I had never experienced such hospitality. The Italians were sincerely warm inviting, and just seemed to have this endless zest for life. We had such an amazing time and I could tell Ellen and I were starting to get close. After a nice dinner and more drinks, we decided we would head back to the hotel. Tomorrow, we will head to the great city of Rome.

When we arrived back at the hotel, everyone was very tired. Ellen and I said goodnight. She went up the stairs to the second floor where she shared a room with Judy and Cynthia. My room was on the first floor, so it was just a quick walk down the hall. Lying in bed that night, I could not help thinking about the great time I had been having since meeting Ellen. I fell asleep with pleasant thoughts of my experiences.

The next morning, we all met in the hotel restaurant for a quick breakfast, and, of course, fresh ground coffee. Ellen was like me in that she loved her first coffee in the morning. After breakfast, we decided rather than drag our luggage through the streets again, we would take the short taxi ride over to the train station.

The train to Rome would take about three hours, and since Ellen and I both had a good night's sleep, we spent the time getting to know each other. As I was now very comfortable with Ellen, I decided it was time to tell her about my boys. Of course, I was somewhat hesitant, as I was not sure if that would scare her off.

"Hey, I have wanted to tell you something," I said.

"You're married," joked Ellen.

"No, no, I really am divorced, I promise you that. However, I should have told you in Venice. I have two sons. Brett and Brandon. Brett is seven, and Brandon is five. They are amazing little guys, and I love them so much," I explained to Ellen.

"Oh, that's wonderful, you could have told me. Were you worried what I would think or something?" said Ellen.

"Yeah, I guess I was afraid it would scare you off," I said, feeling rather embarrassed.

Ellen thought for a second and said, Well, it doesn't. I love children."

A big sigh of relief came over me. I'm not sure why it was such a big deal to me. We just met, and we might never see each other after our time together in Italy. Why was this remotely a concern?

We spent the rest of the time talking. I asked Ellen more about her life. I discovered that Ellen was in corporate sales, not surprising, based on her vibrant and confident personality. She was a Sales Executive for SONY Music, and from what I could tell, she was quite successful. She owned her own condominium in San Diego.

Ellen grew up in Stony Brook, NY, a small town on the north shore of Long Island. Although I visited NYC when I was in college, I had never been to Long Island and did not know much about it. I would discover that Ellen's mom was divorced when Ellen was in college, and later moved to San Diego with her eleven-year-old sister Carole and older sister Gwen. Ellen moved out to San Diego in her early twenties.

Ellen went on to tell me more about her life in San Diego.

I could just tell by looking at Ellen that she was athletic and would discover she enjoyed yoga, running, rollerblading, and anything outdoors. I started to feel exhausted just listening to her. "OMG," I thought to myself. "I'm not sure I can keep up with this girl's endless energy level." I thought I was high energy, but compared to Ellen, I was a bit of a slug.

As we talked more, Ellen told me about a past relationship she had. She was apparently dating a guy, and it must have been very serious because I could tell it was still very painful for Ellen to talk about. Somewhere along the line, as they were contemplating marriage, the guy broke it off. I do not know exactly what happened, and I got the feeling Ellen did not want to get into those details. Ellen said it took her a while to get over, and in her own words, Ellen summarized it by saying, "I put my family through hell for the better part of a year."

As we talked more, I found out that Ellen was raised Jewish. I did not get the sense that Ellen was overly religious, but culturally Judaism was extremely important to her. I did not know much about the Jewish faith, and honestly, until meeting Ellen, I did not have the opportunity to associate with Jewish people. Though raised Catholic, I had no issue dating someone of a different faith.

Ellen talked more about herself, and I could tell that her

social life was extremely important to her. She had many friends and very much valued her social interactions. Now, this did give me pause a bit. It was not as if I was anti-social or anything, but I was certainly not hyper-social; the category I considered for Ellen.

I recalled a couple of years prior; I was dating a beautiful young woman I met in Chicago. We had lots of fun together; however, after about five months, I broke it off as I felt like I was dating her entire family. Everywhere we went; her family had to come with us. Every event had to include her sister, cousins, and extended family. Although I cared for her deeply, it was not a cultural fit, and we were not compatible.

I shared more about my life and told Ellen about my marriage and divorce. I was careful not to get into all the gory details of what led up to the divorce, as I felt it was too soon and didn't want to turn Ellen off by talking about such things. I did tell her, however, that I was the one who initiated the divorce. I talked more about my sons and about my love for martial arts.

As the train started to pull into Rome, both Ellen and I started to get excited. Spending three hours getting to know each other, I felt very comfortable with Ellen.

"Hey, I was thinking," I said cautiously.

"About?" questioned Ellen.

"I was thinking that maybe we get a room together in Rome," I said with a sheepish grin.

"Now there's an idea," said Ellen.

Ellen did not say yes or no, only that it was an idea. I was not sure if, in her mind, it was a good idea or a bad one. I decided it was a good idea.

Chapter 6

Rome

By the time we arrived in Rome, Ellen and I were feeling very comfortable with each other. I also noticed that both Cynthia and Judy now seemed more comfortable that I had joined their vacation. Who knows? Perhaps behind the scenes, they were perturbed, but they seemed okay with everything.

We had selected a very nice hotel in the central area of Rome where we could get to the main areas we wanted to visit. Italy's capital city is massive, with more than 2.8 million residents. For me, it was a dream come true as growing up, I loved studying the Roman Empire and the power of the ancient Romans. With all the many monuments and ancient structures still standing, it was like we had stepped back in time.

As you could imagine, we all wanted to visit as many "Must See" areas Rome had to offer: The Colosseum, The Forum, Vatican City, Circus Maximus, The Pantheon, and ancient temples. While we were all excited about seeing ancient Rome, we also really wanted to enjoy the great Italian food and culture.

Ellen and I did get a room together. I could tell Ellen was hesitant to share a room with me. After all, we had just met three days prior, and I think Ellen may have been concerned I might think her "easy." Of course, I didn't think that at all. I knew something special was happening. We were so comfortable with each other that sharing a room just seemed natural.

After we checked into the hotel, we went up to our room.

As soon as we opened the door to the room and stepped in, we both looked at each other. The hotel rooms in Europe, although equally expensive as the U.S., are much smaller. There was a full-size bed in this tiny little room, barely enough room to walk around. The bathroom was so small, we would both need to take turns to even brush our teeth. I just shrugged and said, "Oh well, I guess we will make do."

Ellen quickly replied, "Oh no, we won't, get your things, we are going to talk to the hotel manager." Ellen's full personality was shining through. I could see she is a take-charge kind of girl. She knows what she wants, she has extremely high standards, and she is tough as nails. We went back to the hotel front desk. I just stood behind Ellen as I knew she planned to do all the talking. After about five minutes, the hotel manager produced keys to a new room and off we went.

I said to Ellen, "What happened?"

"We got a much bigger room on a higher floor, with a better view," Ellen replied.

"Ok, but how much more is it going to cost us," I asked.

"Same price," said Ellen.

When we got up to the room, it was exactly as Ellen described. I mean it wasn't huge but much better than the first room.

Admittedly, I felt a little uncomfortable that I didn't take charge like that, but I was also quite impressed. I was amazed by how sharp Ellen was, her confidence, and her innate ability to take charge.

After everyone got settled into the hotel, we all met in the lobby to make our plans for dinner. Cynthia and Judy, always adventurous, were excited about checking out the nightlife in Rome and finding a great place to get an authentic Roman dinner. We spent some time talking to the concierge and got some ideas on what direction to go. Out the door, we went to explore the beautiful city of Rome!

The Spanish Steps

After walking for a bit, we came upon a huge square that was buzzing with activity. We had found our way to the famous Spanish Steps. The Spanish Steps is something I had read about. Visitors from all over the world had gathered on these steps since the early 1700s. It was a place to socialize, take in the sights, and rest our weary traveling legs.

When Ellen and I got to the Steps, we could see the largest steps in all of Europe were full of people walking up and down, resting, and taking pictures of the historical steps. Many couples sat quietly embracing, enjoying the romance Rome had to offer. Seemingly, out of nowhere, a young man came up to Ellen and presented her with a beautiful rose.

Ellen said, "No, thank you," and started to walk away.

Ellen, being a very savvy salesgirl, knew the rose was going to cost me even though the guy said, "Free, for your beautiful lady."

But good ole gullible John, who thought perhaps it was Rome's gift to tourists, said, "Yes, I will take a rose for the lady."

Then the guy leaned in quickly and said very sternly in my ear, "$10". I paid the guy, and down the steps, we went.

Ellen said, "That was sweet, but you got played."

I blushed, and with a grin, I said, "Yes, I did, but you do look quite stunning with your rose."

We walked down the steps and even sat for a while. It was a great place to people-watch and just enjoy being in Rome I have been to some amazing cities on this trip but there was something special about Rome, and it was quickly becoming one of my favorite places.

The Trevi Fountain

After leaving the steps, we walked what seemed like a brief fifteen minutes and came upon a remarkable site. We had found our way to The Trevi Fountain, one of the most famous fountains in all the world. When we arrived, it wasn't too busy. While there were certainly a lot of tourists, we were able to get right up to the fountain's edge. I had never seen such a fountain – it was simply magnificent. It was built in the mid-1700s, it stands 86ft high and is over 160ft wide. Water pours out from the center of the fountain into a huge pool where people have stood around the edge to gaze at its beauty for 250 years. Beautiful statues decorate the front of the fountain, which reminded me of mythological gods and goddesses.

I had heard it was a myth that if you stand with your back to the fountain and throw a coin over your left shoulder, it would guarantee a return to Rome someday. So of course, Ellen and I did exactly that, then laughed and gave each other a loving hug.

When we got back to our room, we were feeling good about our first day in Rome. We had a wonderful time, and we were looking forward to spending some personal time with each other. You would think it would be awkward between us, but it really felt quite natural.

Ellen went into the bathroom first, and changed her clothes, took off her makeup, and brushed her teeth. A few minutes later, she came out. She was wearing adorable little night shorts and a tank top. I guess I was just staring at her because she looked so cute. She said, "What"? "Oh, nothing", I replied and snuck past her and into the bathroom. I washed up, brushed my teeth, and put on some basic gym shorts and tee shirt. I certainly wasn't expecting a romantic interlude on this trip and only had enough clothes that would fit into a backpack for three weeks. I'm sure when I came out of the bathroom, I wasn't looking overly sexy or anything.

I was a bit nervous as I wasn't sure if I should make the first romantic move. The room was half lit, and Ellen had already secured her side of the bed (closest to the bathroom) and was sitting upright on top of the bedspread. I gently snuggled my way onto the bed, and we immediately kissed passionately while we embraced. The rest of the evening was quite special, and I believe both felt content. It was amazing how comfortable we felt with one another; as if we had known each other for years.

The Colosseum

In the morning, I was the first to wake and was as quiet as possible so as not to disturb Ellen. Similar to my father, I have never required a lot of sleep and get by nicely on six hours a night. I snuck into the bathroom where I could turn on the light, and I just sat on the floor reading my Rome travel book. Today, we were going to visit the world-famous Colosseum. You develop certain perceptions of things you see in movies or read about in books. I had just seen The Gladiator starring Russell Crowe and loved it. Ellen woke up about thirty minutes later and I went over and climbed back into bed with her. It was all so very natural, and neither of us felt weird or anything. We just started to plan out our day together. First, we would get ready and meet the girls in the lobby for breakfast before heading out for the day.

After breakfast, we took a taxi over to the main area where the Colosseum was. In my mind, anyway, I always thought The Colosseum would be out in the country somewhere isolated from the rest of Rome. I was surprised to find out that modern Rome had just built itself up and around ancient Rome, with cars buzzing all around the ancient structure. As we walked up to the front of the massive structure, it was amusing to see guys dressed up as ancient Roman Gladiators, fully equipped with their armor and swords. Of course, they were there for the entertainment of the tourists waiting in line, and for a few bucks, you could get your picture taken with one of the gladiators. I thought for a second that I should go up and throw a Kung Fu kick at one of the gladiators, then I thought, knowing my luck, I might get my leg, or something else, cut off by a Roman sword.

As Ellen and I were waiting in line, one couldn't help but look at the magnificent amphitheater. I was thinking it must have been an extraordinary construction project in its day, almost 2,000 years ago. I wonder what it was like back in 80 A.D. when it was completed. At its peak, the Colosseum could hold 80,000 spectators. I found that to be quite impressive. We finally made it through the doors, and we were inside the massive structure, yet very much on the outskirts of the main floor. It reminded me of modern-day football stadiums where the concession stands are on the outskirts of the arena.

Ellen and I followed the crowd up the stairs and into the main body of The Colosseum. The stadium seating, while in decline, was still there.

After all, the structure was made of limestone and concrete so it obviously could withstand the ages. The seats, also like today's standards, had the more expensive seating closer to the floor, and the nosebleed sections went all the way to the top of the amphitheater. There were countless archways spread across the stadium where I assumed spectators could pass from the main body to the outer sections of the structure. As we looked at the floor of The Colosseum, it was noticeable that they only had half of the floor intact so you could see the many lower levels. We discovered by reading some of the kiosks that the lower levels were where the gladiators and many varieties of animals were kept for entertainment purposes. The emperors of the day would stage magnificent shows to commemorate battles won. Gladiators would fight to the death to entertain the crowd.

Ellen and I spent about an hour walking around The Colosseum, took some great pictures, and then made our way to the exit. We both knew we had just experienced something quite exceptional and as we walked, we reflected on our travel back in time.

Vatican City

For me, touring Vatican City was an extremely emotional experience. A city-state and the center of the Catholic faith, with 1.3 billion Catholics from around the world, it was just amazing to see. While we walked through the holy city, I knew it probably did not mean as much to Ellen as it did to me. However, we both were in awe at the grandeur of it all, and I was happy to be able to enjoy it with Ellen.

St. Peter's Basilica, which took over one hundred years to build, was completed in 1626. I had many of the same emotions as when we walked through St. Mark's in Venice, yet St. Peter's was even more impressive. The structure itself was just massive, not sure, but seemed to be almost twice the size of St. Mark's. Named after The Apostle Peter and the place of his burial, St. Peter's is the largest church in the world, at least of the Christian faith.

The experience of walking through The Vatican was amazing on multiple levels. There was the cathedral, and there was also a museum of some of the finest paintings and sculptures the world has ever known. It is the place of worship of the Pope and many of the Catholic clergy from all over the world who come to visit. It was the heart of the Catholic faith, and I was there to see it.

While I literally had tears rolling down my face, overcome with emotion and joy, Ellen had quite a different experience. She had commented that all the paintings and sculptures look the same. "Seems like just a bunch of nude people, everything looks the same," remarked Ellen. I wished Ellen could see and experience what I did. However, I surmsised, by not having a Christian background, maybe she could not fully appreciate the historical significance of it all.

Having Ellen with me sped things up quite a bit, as she was not interested in stopping and reading about everything. We walked through the entire facility though, and ended up at the amazing Sistine Chapel. We walked through this normal-sized door, and suddenly, I was astonished to see we had just walked into the main body of the magnificent Sistine Chapel. It seemed like two hundred people were standing in the center of this huge room, all looking straight up sixty-eight feet to the ceiling. I don't think I have ever seen such man-made beauty. Now I'm certainly no art expert, but I did take an intense art class in college, and the work of the Vatican was a major subject of study.

One of the most well-known pieces of art I recognized immediately was the Last Judgment by Michelangelo. Other ceiling paintings included other prominent Renaissance artists such as Sandro Botticelli, Pietro Perugino, Pinturicchio, and Domenico Ghirlandaio. I literally could have stayed in the chapel for hours, but Ellen and I felt the pressure of hundreds of other tourists behind us all waiting their turn, so we followed the stream of people out through the many corridors until we found ourselves outside of the Vatican.

We had been in Rome for three full days, and our time there was quickly coming to an end. I still had another week left in my journey and was planning to go spend a couple of days in Naples before heading to Greece to finish out my adventure. Ellen, Judy, and Cynthia only had a couple of days left in Europe and were planning to head to Florence next for a quick visit before going back up to Zurich to catch their flight back to the U.S.

Ellen and I had such a nice time together in Venice, Bologna, and Rome; we were saddened at the thought of leaving each other. As we were contemplating saying goodbye, Ellen said rather enthusiastically, "I know, I have an idea. What if I don't go to Florence and instead go to Naples with you? I can meet up with Cynthia and Judy in a couple of days."

I was delighted with Ellen's creative thinking and said, "That's the best news I've heard all day."

Chapter 7

Naples and 9/11

It took just under three hours to get to Naples from Rome. As we were on the train, I was thinking about why I selected Naples as one of my key European destinations. In doing research on my family history, my ancestors on my father's side immigrated to the United States in the mid to late 1800s. I thought it would be interesting to explore my roots a little and see the area where my great-grandparents lived.

When we arrived in Naples, honestly, the area around the train station looked a little seedy. Perhaps I was being overly cautious, but my sixth sense, as they call it in martial arts, was telling me to be extra aware of my surroundings. It just did not seem safe. At one point, I was waiting for Ellen while she stopped to use the bathroom. I was intently looking at a map of Naples with my back turned to the main part of the terminal.

Something told me to look over my shoulder, and sure enough, a pickpocket was on a direct course, walking quickly and reaching out to snatch my passport, which I carelessly left hanging out of my back pocket. I turned quickly, was now facing the man directly, and gave him the most penetrating look possible, demonstrating it was best he does not mess with me. The man quickly veered off and tried to act as if he was just walking naturally through the station.

It was about a ten-minute taxi ride over to our hotel from Naples Central Station. We picked a modest hotel near Castel Sant'Elmo, a 13th-century castle-like fortress.

Ellen and I were standing at the front desk checking into our hotel when suddenly a woman rushed over to me, grabbed my arm, and with a look of horror on her face screamed, "Are you Americans?"

I said, "Yes."

With a heavy Italian accent, she said, "You must come see." She still had me by the arm and led me into a separate room off the lobby. Ellen was close behind us, and as we entered the room, we could see a crowd of people standing in front of the lobby television; some were crying frantically, so I knew whatever they were watching was not good news.

As Ellen and I watched the news broadcast, we could see one of the towers of the World Trade Center in New York City was on fire. As we continued to watch, we saw an airplane fly into the second tower.

It was September 11, 2001, a date to forever remember. America was under attack, seemingly by terrorists. As we continued to watch the devastation, we were in shock. Both of us were from New York and had friends and family there. We did not know what to do.

The Italians there were extremely comforting. Many of them came up to Ellen and me and expressed their sincere sympathy and support. One man said, "We stand with America." While Ellen and I were frightened, we felt the love from the Italians, which did provide comfort.

After watching the broadcast for another fifteen minutes, we went back to the lobby and finished checking in. We went right to our room to see if we could get in touch with our families in the U.S. We decided we would take turns trying to call out.

Ellen went first and tried calling her mom. All the phone lines were jammed, and it took a good twenty minutes for the lines to connect, but finally, Ellen reached her mom. Ellen was very close to her mother, Florence, and I could tell by the look on her face she was relieved to know that she was okay.

They talked for a few minutes as Ellen was trying to find out what was going on. After some time, I motioned to Ellen to finish the call so I could see if I could check in on my kids and my parents. Ellen said, "Ok, mom, I need to go now, John needs to call his parents. I will call you later. Love you."

It took me equally long to get in touch with my parents. My father answered the phone, and we talked only briefly. My main concern was to make sure everyone in our family was safe. My father confirmed what he knew from watching the news. Our country was attacked by terrorists who hijacked commercial airplanes and flew them into the World Trade Center and The Pentagon.

In his usual way, my father had a way of comforting me and just said, "Everything is going to be fine. Just stay safe out there."

I then called my ex-wife to check on Brett and Brandon. They were glad to hear from me; and being so young, they really did not know what was going on. Their mother told me they were fine.

After Ellen and I made our calls back to the U.S., we just sat there looking at one another. We were shocked and extremely worried about our country. I personally felt guilty that I was not home and felt like I should be doing something. I said to Ellen, "Now, what do we do?"

Ellen said, "Well, there really isn't anything we do at this point. Let's just enjoy the rest of our vacation." It turns out that Ellen has this amazing way of compartmentalizing. Though she was no doubt concerned and worried, her position was to continue to enjoy our last day together and explore Naples.

I snapped back, "Enjoy our vacation? How are we going to enjoy our vacation when our country is under attack?" Ellen responded in a stern voice, "John, there is nothing we can do right now from here. Tomorrow, we must leave here. You are going to Greece, and I am going to Florence. Let's get something to eat and see some of the sights."

It was the first time since we met when Ellen and I were not aligned. However, after I sat there and thought about it a bit, I realized we were both afraid for our country and worried about our families. Of course, it was reasonable to expect us to be frustrated and anxious.

After a few more minutes, I realized Ellen was right, and I agreed to try my best to enjoy the day. Naples is the third largest city in Italy after Rome and Milan, so there was a lot to explore in the short amount of time we had.

After talking to the front desk clerk about where we might go, he suggested we visit Castel dell'Ovo, an ancient seaside castle. Our hotel was a short walk from the castle, so we started to head in the direction of the sea, as suggested by the hotel manager.

Ellen and I were both getting hungry, so we decided to stop and have a nice lunch before exploring the castle. We found a little place that served pizza, and let me tell you, it was the best pizza we had ever eaten. We enjoyed the amazing pizza and had a couple of beers. We slowly started to try to put what was happening back in the States to the side for a brief period.

From there, we explored Castel dell'Ovo, the largest and oldest structure in Naples, built by the Normans in the 12th century. It was awesome to see. Naples is a massive city, and we knew there were so many other points of interest, churches, catacombs, shoreline cruises. However, neither of us had the motivation to do those things given the horrible terrorist attacks back home.

From the Castle, we just decided to stroll leisurely through some of the city streets before heading back to our hotel. Once back at the hotel, we caught up on the news from the hotel lobby television. It was devastating to think of the senseless loss of lives at the hands of murderous radicals. Why would anyone want to do such a thing to our country, to innocent men, women, and children?

New York City was in shambles, the World Trade Center towers had been completely leveled, and the death toll was rising. After a modest dinner at a nearby restaurant, we went back to our room and went to bed relatively early.

The next morning, Ellen and I were saddened by the terrorist attacks and the fact that we needed to go our separate ways. However, we knew that meeting each other was something to be cherished. While we were not exactly sure if we would see each other again, we did discuss the possibility of getting together when we were back in the United States; something that would be logistically challenging with Ellen living in San Diego, and me in Chicago. We figured we would somehow work it out.

We enjoyed a late breakfast together at the hotel and then did some more exploring of Naples. After several hours, we made our way back to the hotel and checked out and headed for the airport.

As we were evaluating the train schedules, Ellen's train to Florence, where she would reconnect with Cynthia and Judy, would leave before my train to Brindisi.

As the time approached for Ellen to leave, I walked her to her platform, where the train was already there, and people were starting to board. As we stood on the platform, we were both very quiet, not really knowing what to say to each other.

To my surprise, Ellen said, "I have something for you." She reached into her bag and pulled out a little picture book of Rome and handed it to me. She said, "I know how much you loved Rome and thought you might like this as something to remember our time together." The book was entitled Rome Past & Present.

As I opened the book, I could see Ellen wrote me a nice message, which said, "John, it's been a wonderful 6 days together! I have totally enjoyed our trip together through Italy. Io ero essere pensare di lei."

I had to hold back my tears. I was so impressed that she thought to give me a parting gift. I should have done something like that.

I said, "Ellen, thank you so much, I absolutely love this."

***The book Ellen gave me as we said goodbye to
each other at the train station in Naples***

***The inside cover of the book was inscribed by
Ellen***

It was now time for Ellen to board the train. We gave each other a big hug and a brief kiss. I helped her get her luggage on board and jumped off the train. I was watching Ellen as she took a window seat on the train. A few minutes later, the train began to slowly depart. Ellen was waving from the window and gave me that same beautiful smile that stopped me in my tracks when we first met just six days prior. I felt this pit in my stomach as if I was going to be sick as she faded into the distance. I immediately wondered to myself why I did not just go with her to Florence. However, I also really wanted to see Greece and who knows when I would get this opportunity again.

With Ellen now on her way to reconnect with her friends in Florence, I was feeling very much alone, but I was determined to push forward and finish out the rest of the journey I had planned. I did not have to wait long before my train left for Brindisi. It was going to take about five hours to get to Brindisi. I boarded quickly, and as the train started to pull away from Naples, the thought of the terrorist attacks came over me, and I became somewhat anxious, and afraid.

The senseless loss of life weighed heavily upon me. Now, well, on my way to Brindisi, I spent the time looking out the window and reflecting upon my time with Ellen. I opened the little book about Rome that Ellen gave me and started sifting through the pages. I was looking through my Italian phrase book to try to figure out how to translate what Ellen wrote in Italian. I surmised either it meant, "I will be thinking of you," or perhaps, "I hope you will be thinking of me." Either way, it tugged on my heartstrings. Though my experience with Ellen was difficult to comprehend, I could not help but think that I needed to see her again someday. Before we left each other, Ellen told me that when she called her very Jewish mother to report in, she had told her about meeting me.

"Mom, I met this guy," said Ellen.

"Ok……." said Florence (Flo).

"He's from Chicago," Ellen said enthusiastically.

"Oh, Chicago. That's nice," Flo listened intently.

"He's divorced," Ellen hesitated slightly before completing the description.

"Divorced, ok, well, he's at least single," said Flo.

"He has two kids, and he's Catholic," Ellen finally blurted out.

"Oy Vey……well, I'm sure it is just a little summertime romance, right?" said Florence.

Ellen had told me she was very close to her mother. Florence's faith in Judaism was a fundamental part of her being. I'm sure she was none too happy that her little girl met a Catholic. I didn't get a chance to find out too much about Ellen's father other than he was now remarried. As the sound of the train gently comforted me into a light sleep, I wondered if this was just a fling, as Ellen's mom suggested, or perhaps the start of a longer-lasting relationship. Time will tell.

Chapter 8

Brindisi

Brindisi is a small seaport in the southeast of the country, on the edge of the Adriatic Sea; considered to be the 'Gateway to Greece.' Most people know that Italy is shaped like a boot. Brindisi is in the heel of the boot, almost the furthest south you can go in that part of Italy. In planning my trip, Brindisi was always just a place I would pass through on my way from Italy to Greece. I never intended it to be a destination where I would spend much time exploring, so I really did not do a lot of research on Brindisi. The train dropped me off in an area called Piazza Francesco Crispi on the southwest side of the city around 11:00 PM.

The distance between the train station and the Ferry Port was less than an hour's walk. I had decided I would just start walking and head in the direction of the seaport, where I would find a hotel for the night. The ferry I selected to take me to Greece did not leave until very late the next day, so I checked into a hotel and went right to sleep. My thought was that the next day, I would just wander around and see the sites as I did not have much of a plan. I knew I wanted to be at the Ferry Port early to give me plenty of time before the ferry left for Patras, Greece.

The next morning, I found a place to have a less-than-exciting breakfast and ventured out for some exploring. I found my way to some monument celebrating Italian soldiers and discovered Castello Svevo di Brindisi, a huge 13th-century castle that was closed to the public since it is still used as a military building. It was still quite impressive to see it from the outside. I boarded the ferry around 6:30 PM; the journey to Patras, Greece, would be about sixteen hours, so we would be traveling through the night. It was going to be quite a journey to the port of Greece at Patras. I was getting conflicting information on how long it would take, but over fifteen hours. We left in the early evening, and the ferry would pull into Patras around noon the next day.

I checked on sleeping accommodations and concluded they were just too expensive. I was running low on funds and did not want to run up a huge credit card bill, so I figured I would just sleep sitting upright in a standard seat. I found a comfortable seat and stared out at the beautiful ocean as the little ferry chugged its way toward Greece. As sunset, I decided it was time for an adult beverage and grabbed a beer and a turkey sandwich from the little bar area that was set up.

I then headed out to the deck, where about ten guys were just hanging out and talking. To my surprise, they were all quite inviting and asked me to join them. It turns out they were all Germans on holiday. Every one of them spoke perfect English, and they knew more about US politics and history than I did. I was feeling a little bit inadequate in terms of how worldly they were compared to me.

They were all so nice and asked an abundance of questions. They had a sincere and genuine interest in the United States and Americans in general. They were specifically inquisitive about the girls in the United States.

"Well, let me tell you about this little doll from San Diego I just met in Venice."

They all got a kick out of my story. I returned the conversation, asking them about life in Germany. We did not discuss WWII or the holocaust or anything quite so complicated. It was more about our cultures, interests, and lifestyles. I had such a great time, and we talked for hours. I lost track of what time it was until I started to see the sun come up. The sun began to glisten on the ocean surface, I could feel the mist of the ocean and the warmth of the sun on my face. It was really quite spectacular. We all went in for some coffee as we were almost in Patras. I was so grateful for the opportunity to meet my new friends.

Chapter 9

Greece

Once I disembarked from the ferry, I realized I had not really mapped out how I was getting to Athens. My options were taxi, train, or bus. As I was trying to figure out what I was going to do, I came upon a group of young Australian men on holiday.

One of the young men must have noticed I was traveling alone and yelled over to me, "How goes it, mate? Seems you might be going our way; welcome to join us if ya like."

I was so happy he invited me along with them, and I quickly walked over to him, offered him my hand, and said, "I would love to; I'm John from Chicago."

The man smiled and said, "Glad to meet you, John from Chicago, James from Broome." He then introduced me to six of his friends. As luck would have it, they were also heading to Athens and were heading to the bus station, where we would take the 2.5-3.0-hour bus ride into Athens. That sounded fine to me. It was great to meet new friends. It was so refreshing to be able to just go with the flow and take advantage of opportunities that came up. The Australians were all good-natured and fun-loving guys, all just out to enjoy their holiday, see new sights, and meet new people.

I thought one of the guys referred to it as a walk-about or

something, but maybe I got that wrong. Anyway, seems like most people I met outside of the United States don't refer to travel as "vacation." They generally refer to it as "going on holiday." Everyone was very nice to me and asked me many questions about the United States and the great city of Chicago. Like the Germans I spent time with on the ferry from Brindisi, I was extremely impressed with their knowledge of the United States.

When we got on the bus, I sat next to James. I had never been to Australia, and sadly, my only reference to Australians was Crocodile Dundee. Thinking I was being clever and travel smart, I brought up Mick Dundee and the popular movie Crocodile Dundee. I loved the movie, mostly because of Linda Kozlowski. To my surprise James just rolled his eyes, smiled, and said, "Mate, let me tell ya something. Aussies hate that movie. Really puts us all in a bad light, you get my meaning?"

Trying to cover up my ignorance, I just said, "Sorry, bud, yes, I know what you mean." James and I had a great time chatting most of the three-hour bus ride to Athens.

Athens

When we arrived at the bus station in Athens, it became apparent that my Australian friends were only going to be in Athens for a brief period and then heading north to explore Mt. Olympus. My plans were to hang out in Athens's city center before going out to the Greek island of Mykonos. Therefore, it was time for me to say goodbye to my friends. Though we had only spent 4-5 hours together, I really felt a connection with them. After shaking hands and extending some pleasantries, I watched them all walk away with backpacks secured, laughing and joking just like when I first met them back in Brindisi. It made me smile.

I found my way to where the taxis were all waiting. In Athens, it did not seem like many of the taxi drivers spoke English. I walked from driver to driver, trying to find someone who would at least try to engage with me. I found a young driver who spoke a little English. I had the address of my hotel written out, and he nodded as if he knew where it was. He quickly popped open his trunk for my backpack, I got in, and we went speeding off through the streets of Athens. Athens is a monstrous, sprawling city.

Unlike my past destinations where I could at least make out some of the street signs, in Athens, well, it was all Greek to me. I was quite literally at the mercy of my driver. As we were driving, I was just looking out the window at all the cars and buses speeding in every direction. The people of Athens were carrying on with their business. There seemed to be a high energy in the city. It may have taken only ten minutes to get to my hotel. We pulled up to what seemed to be a very modest hotel, a location I picked relatively close to the Acropolis, which was the primary attraction I wanted to see. I quickly checked into the hotel, dropped off my stuff, and immediately bolted out the door again after getting some basic directions from the hotel manager.

The Acropolis

I was feeling energetic and excited to experience ancient Greece. Athens seemed a little easier to navigate on foot compared to what I experienced in Venice and Naples. Or maybe it just seemed that way as I was starting to get more comfortable as a tourist. The walk up to the Acropolis seemed to take a while and it was a steady incline to get to the top. When I got to the top of the ancient hill, I just stood there in awe. I was standing in the same place where the ancient Greeks stood more than 3,000 years ago. I recalled from my research and some of the classes I took in college that the Acropolis was originally built by the ancients during the reign of Pericles (c. 495-429 BC) as a fortress and military base, sitting high on the hill it was used to protect the people of Athens.

I walked around the entire complex, taking pictures of the beautiful buildings and statues. It was hard for me to take it all in at first. To think that the United States was just over two hundred years old, and the ancient Greeks walked this land thousands of years ago. I found myself standing in front of the Parthenon, the finest temple in the ancient world. The Parthenon was built approximately 2500 years ago as a temple of the goddess Athena. While the temple was mostly in ruins now due to the impacts of war and time, it was still a remarkable structure that served multiple purposes over the centuries.

I couldn't help thinking that Ellen would really enjoy seeing this and thought it would have been nice if she was there with me. I walked the ancient grounds from the Parthenon and stopped in front of the magnificent marble temple named the Erechtheion, dedicated to Athena and Zeus. The temple displayed Six Beautiful Maidens (Caryatids of Erechtheion), which are beautiful female statues that serve as columns to the ancient porch.

My travel book said the maidens were considered one of the most sacred areas of the Acropolis. Once I had finished exploring the Acropolis, I walked about a quarter of a mile southwest to Filoppapos Hill. I had timed it exactly right as the sun was starting to set, and from the hill, I had an amazing view of Athens. I just sat for some time looking out over the city and fantasized about what it must have looked like all those centuries ago.

As it was getting darker, I started to head down the hill towards my hotel. I came upon a bar that looked lively and fun. The music was playing loudly, and the place seemed packed, mostly with what looked like locals. I went in and sat down at one of the tables close to the bar and ordered a beer. I was just sitting there listening to music and watching people when I suddenly noticed this young and quite beautiful young woman make her way over to me. I am guessing she was about 22 years old, wearing a short skirt with a low-cut blouse, which displayed her quite perky breasts.

She pulled out the chair and said with a strong accent, "May I sit down."

I said, "Sure."

She introduced herself as Zoe and smiled. I asked her if she was Greek, and she explained that she was from Romania. Before I could say anything else, the bartender came up to me and said, "Would you like to take her home with you? Where is your hotel? She can meet you at your hotel, no problem." I practically spit my beer out of my mouth. The young woman laughed. I felt like the biggest dummy. I was only in Athens for a brief period, and I was being propositioned by a prostitute.

I smiled and said to the man, "No, thank you, sir."

The man said, "What's wrong? Do you not like her, is she not pretty?"

"She is very pretty," but thank you, no," I responded with a smile.

The young woman got up quickly and walked away. The bartender just disappeared back to the bar as if nothing ever happened. I quickly finished my beer and left. I decided to head back to my hotel before I got myself into trouble. Before I got back to my hotel, I picked up fast food and took it back to my room. Even though it was getting late in Athens, it was still early in the day back in Chicago. I called my boys and talked with them for a bit. They were so cute, and I told them all about my travels. After talking to Brett and Brandon, I fell fast asleep, quite tired from a day of touring.

Mykonos

In the morning, I grabbed a light breakfast, checked out of the hotel, and took a taxi to the ferry port. I had decided to head to Mykonos. I had read that Mykonos was quite wild and fun, so I thought that would be a good place to visit for my first Greek island. The ferry was over three hours long. I had no idea it would be that long, but the ride over to the island was beautiful. I spent most of that time just looking out over the water and thinking about how fortunate I was.

When the ferry docked in Mykonos, I took a taxi to my hotel, which wasn't too far away. After checking in and getting my stuff put away in the room, out the door I went and found my way to Agios Stefanos beach, one of the beaches the hotel manager recommended. It was a beautiful day; the sun was high in the sky; the sand on the beach was warm on my feet; but not too hot. The beach was quite crowded, but I was able to find a lounge chair on the beach. I plopped myself down and stretched out. I am not usually one to lay around too long, but I thought I would try to relax after two and a half weeks of intense travel.

I was just sitting there looking around. The sea was stunning, aqua blue, with the sun reflecting a beautiful warm glow. The beautiful white sand beach was packed with people coming and going in every direction. To my pleasant surprise, I noticed that many of the women were just wearing the bottoms of their bikinis. Some of the women (and men) weren't wearing anything at all. The hotel manager had obviously sent me to a clothing-optional beach.

"I'll have to remember to tip that guy when I get back to the hotel," I thought. A few minutes later, two young women arrived and sat in the two lounge chairs to my left that had just become available. Since the beach was so crowded, the chairs were right on top of each other. The women quickly removed their bikini tops and just laid there half-naked.

"I'm really digging Greece," I mumbled to myself. I know I should have felt like I died and went to heaven; however, after about thirty minutes, I started to feel a little sad, as if there was something missing, and in fact, I could not relax no matter how hard I tried. I began reflecting on the six days I spent with Ellen; even though it was a brief encounter, I started to miss her. All these thoughts kept running through my mind.

"Where is she now? Did she make it back to the States ok, was she thinking of me? Will I ever see her again?"

I could not believe it. Here I was in Greece, on the beautiful party island of Mykonos, surrounded by beautiful half-naked women, and all I could do was think about Ellen. I laughed to myself and said aloud, "She ruined the last week of my vacation." The woman with the beautiful naked breasts looked over at me, wondering if I was talking to her. I just smiled. At that moment, I knew what I had to do. I stood up quickly, packed up all my stuff, and left the beach area. I decided I needed to find an internet café and see if I could email Ellen to see how she was doing. Now my next dilemma. I had no idea where I could find an internet café on this little island.

When I was in Athens, I noticed them quite frequently as I was walking around, but here on the island, there was no sign of one. I asked a few locals and finally found a nice man who told me he knew of one, but it was some distance away, and gave me some vague directions on how to get there. I got on this old noisy bus headed in the direction the man explained to me. About twenty minutes later, the bus dropped us off at some central station. Honestly, I had no idea where I was, but I did manage to find the internet café, which was exactly where the nice man had told me. I entered this little café, and paid for my internet session and a cup of coffee.

Let me tell you, the Greeks like their coffee strong. "Probably won't need to sleep again for a few days," I said out loud.

I looked at my email account, hoping there would be an email from Ellen, but sadly, there was no email from her. "That's ok", perhaps she was busy at work just getting back from vacation," I thought to myself. I sat back and practiced in my mind what I might say to her. Then, I started second-guessing myself.

Would she even wish to engage with me any further? Perhaps in her mind, our time together was just a one-time thing. After all, she lives in San Diego, and I live in Chicago. How could that possibly work? I am certainly not moving to California. I have my boys, and I have my career. There would be no way she would move to Chicago. As awesome as Chicago is, who in their right mind would move from 73 degrees and sunny year-round to minus zero wind chills and six months of winter? Oh well, I decided I was certainly going to find out.

I started typing my email to her: "Hi Ellen, hopefully you made it back to San Diego ok. I am on the Greek island of Mykonos. It is beautiful here. I think you would like it. Anyway, I was just thinking of you and wanted to say hello. Write when you can. It might take me a while to respond, as there are very few internet places on this island. Bye for now.......John." Even though I was really missing her, I didn't want to come across as too needy. It was at that point I felt like my European vacation was coming to an end. My heart and mind were just not in it any longer. I needed to figure out what I was going to do about this girl named Ellen, who somehow dropped into my life.

The rest of my stay in Mykonos was uneventful, just kind of meandering around killing time. I checked out of my hotel and headed to the ferry station. During the ferry ride back to Athens, I began to take account of my overall European adventure. For my first time traveling alone, I thought I did well. I didn't make too many horrible mistakes (except for getting intoxicated in Venice), I got to see all my intended sites, plus many others, and more importantly I met someone potentially quite special. From where the ferry dropped me off, I headed directly to the Athens airport via taxi.

Chapter 10

Back in Chicago

When I landed back in Chicago, I made my way to baggage claim. I was exhausted from the long flight and just wanted to see Brett and Brandon. As I walked out to the main area of the terminal at O'Hare, I was surprised to see my ex-wife and my boys standing there. I had given my ex-wife my flight plans so she knew when I would return to Chicago. I thought that it was so nice of her to bring the boys to meet me. I went running up to them and gave them the biggest hug. They were both smiling from ear to ear.

It was Friday, so I would be able to spend the entire weekend with them. I got the boys back to my townhouse, and we ordered pizza for dinner. We played games and wrestled, and the boys took turns jumping from the top of the bunk bed into a pile of blankets. This always made me nervous as I didn't want them to get hurt. Once the boys calmed down and were in bed, I called Ellen. It was two hours earlier in San Diego, and I thought I might catch her at home.

Before I dialed the number, I couldn't help wondering if maybe she was with someone, a boyfriend, or something. After all, I really wasn't sure if our brief time together meant as much to Ellen as it did to me. I was happy when Ellen answered the phone. It was great to hear her voice. I know this may sound silly, but I found Ellen's voice to be comforting and rather sexy. We picked right back up where we left off in Italy and ended up talking for a couple of hours. The following weekend, I didn't have my boys and had made plans to have dinner with Samantha. We went out to a nice restaurant, one we used to go to quite often. Samantha was sweet and was genuinely interested in hearing about my trip. Although she never asked, I'm sure she wondered why I never called her while I was away for three weeks.

I told her about all my experiences traveling from Amsterdam to Greece. As I was telling her more about Venice in particular, I said, "Samantha, do you remember telling me you thought I would meet my life partner on this trip?"

Samantha's smile became more serious, and she said, "And………"

I responded almost apologetically and said, "Well, too soon to know for sure, but I did meet someone very special." Although I didn't get into the details, I did tell Samantha I was with Ellen in Italy for almost a week. I explained that I needed to explore the relationship with Ellen further, and as such, I was not going to date anyone else. Samantha was quite mature about it, and we agreed to be friends. I dropped Samantha off at her place, gave her a big hug, and watched her walk into her apartment. Sadly, we never saw each other again, and talked on the phone just a few times before the relationship faded.

While I'm sure she was happy for me, she probably figured she should spend her time and energy elsewhere. While Ellen and I had not really talked about being exclusive, I decided I was going to act as if we were. I had a couple of other female friends I would see occasionally, and I called each of them and explained that I was now in a relationship and would not be able to see them any longer. During the following weeks, I focused on work and spending time with my boys.

I found divorce with small children quite challenging. I always felt guilty because I wasn't happy in the marriage, and my children had to become accustomed to living in both places. My youngest, Brandon seemed to adapt more easily, and when it was my weekend, I could tell he was happy to come to spend time with his dad. Brett had it a little harder and sometimes didn't want to come. This was very upsetting to me and added to my already mounting guilt.

We eventually worked through it, and my ex-wife and I developed a workable and cordial relationship focused on raising the children. When it was my time with the boys, I would focus on just them. We would go to Chucky Cheese for pizza and games, go to the amusement park in Gurnee, IL (Great America), and hang out at my townhouse. Overall, I believe I was a good dad, but I definitely had my moments when I wasn't at my best.

I remember a particular incident when I was picking up my boys at my ex-wife's house, that was quite disastrous. I had this old Chevy Blazer, which I used to tow the boat that my ex-wife and I had when we were married. When picking up the boys, I was in a bit of a hurry, and I left the truck running but somehow locked the keys in. After picking up the boys, I went out to the truck to find it running and locked. I didn't know what to do. My ex-wife was standing in the doorway, and my kids were standing there waiting to get in the truck.

Without hesitation, I asked the boys to go stand by their mom, I then picked up a huge rock that lined the driveway and heaved it through the window. I then wiped away all of the glass and said nonchalantly, "Ok, boys, jump on in…..time to spend some fun time with the old man."

Brandon and Brett both laughed and climbed up into the truck. Off we went down the street with the broken window and all with me waiving out the window to the boy's mom. I looked back at my ex-wife and smiled— she just glared at me as if to say, "You're an idiot."

Chapter 11
Two Thousand Miles Between Us

In the following days, Ellen and I talked on the phone every night after work, and although it was difficult not to be with each other physically, it was those phone calls that allowed us to get to know each other. We enjoyed talking with each other, we had similar interests, and our conversations always flowed naturally. The one thing that stood out to me was the way we solved problems together.

Ellen was a great sounding board for me regarding my children and my career. She genuinely cared about my boys and was always thinking of their best interests. She was supportive of my career and always provided that emotional lift if I had a challenging day. Although it was too soon to talk about anything serious, we were very much looking forward to seeing each other, which we had planned for the second weekend after returning from Italy.

We decided I would be the first to venture out, and we planned my trip to see Ellen in San Diego. Ellen found it odd that I had been to Europe, Canada, Mexico, Jamaica, Hawaii, etc., but I had never been to California. I told her I never had the opportunity or need. For my first visit, we decided I would take a long weekend, fly out on Friday, and fly back to Chicago on Monday. The flight was only a little over four hours, so it wasn't too bad. Upon landing in San Diego, I couldn't believe how close the planes flew over the downtown buildings.

The view of the ocean was stunning with that beautiful Southern California sun shining brightly off the water below. I could see huge boats docked in the marinas. I had heard San Diego was beautiful, but I didn't realize it would be this nice. "No wonder Ellen likes it here," I thought to myself. I got off the plane, and quickly made my way to the baggage claim area, where Ellen said she would be waiting for me. As I headed down the escalator, I panned the entire area, and sure enough, there was Ellen. Her eyes were already fixated on me, and she gave me that most awesome smile. She looked amazing, wearing cute little shorts and a pretty blouse. We gave each other the most passionate hug and a little kiss on the lips.

Upon leaving the airport, I couldn't believe how warm it was in San Diego in October. When we got out to the airport parking garage, I was impressed that Ellen drove a very sporty maroon-colored Jeep Liberty. I laughed to myself as I thought that was cool. Ellen drove me to her condo which was about twenty minutes from the airport. She lived in beautiful Del Mar. As I stepped into her condo, I thought, "Wow, this girl must be doing pretty well for herself."

I figured that, as high-energy and smart as she was, there was no doubt that she was an excellent sales executive. Her place was small but still spacious, especially for one person, and it was nicely decorated and remarkably clean. I was thinking, "When she comes to visit me in Chicago, I better step up my game and maybe hire a cleaning crew or something." During that short weekend, Ellen and I covered a lot of ground. She showed me all over San Diego: We drove down Highway 101 and passed by all the beautiful beaches from Torrey Pines, through Solana Beach, Del Mar, Encinitas, and Carlsbad. It was simply postcard beautiful.

Ellen took me to La Jolla, where we watched the sea lions bask in the sun on the beach. We rollerbladed around Mission Bay, rented bikes, had drinks at cafes on the water, and we had an absolute blast together. Ellen was extremely athletic and coordinated. She was doing laps around me while we were blading. This girl had so much energy, I wasn't sure if she was from this world or an alien that landed on Earth by accident. After hours of physical activity, we enjoyed a nice dinner out, then went back to Ellen's place. After a day with Ellen, I was exhausted. It was as if we were back in Italy. Everything seemed so comfortable, so natural.

During the rest of the weekend, I met Ellen's mom, Flo, and her two sisters Carole and Gwen, and their families. I also had the chance to meet Ellen's best friend Carol, an extremely fun person, pretty, smart, and a high-energy kind of gal. I learned that Ellen and Carol were long-time friends and had traveled all over together. Ellen talked fondly about her travels with Carol and all their countless adventures. I wasn't exactly sure what Ellen had told everyone about me, but they were all very nice and welcoming.

When it was time for me to head back to Chicago, Ellen, and I both became very sad. We were getting closer, and we both knew it was special. The distance between San Diego and Chicago was a huge dark cloud over our heads. How in the world could we make this work? We decided to take one day at a time. Ellen dropped me off at the airport. We hugged each other closely, both with tears in our eyes. We agreed we would meet next in Chicago in a month. I stood there outside of the airport and watched her drive away. Over the next four weeks, Ellen and I continued to talk almost nightly on the phone. Our conversations continued to grow more intimate, and we were falling more in love with each passing day.

It was early, just before Halloween, when Ellen arrived in Chicago. I picked her up at O'Hare and took her back to my place. After my divorce, I purchased a nice townhome in the northern Chicago suburbs in an area called Grayslake. After Ellen unpacked her suitcase and got settled a bit from the long flight, I took her for a drive and showed her some of Chicago's northern suburbs (Grayslake, Gurnee, Waukegan, etc.). We eventually found our way further south and passed by Northbrook, where I pointed out Allstate Insurance Company, where I worked.

After a while, Ellen asked if Lake Michigan was close as she heard there were some beautiful communities off the lake. I said, "Sure, there are several cities that make up what we refer to as the North Shore. Let's go". Over the next couple of hours, we passed through the communities of Skokie, Glencoe, Glenview, and a few others. When we got to the city of Highland Park, Ellen asked if we could stop and walk around. She was quite impressed with the little town.

It was charming and had a beautiful, quaint downtown area. Close by was a rather popular outdoor musical festival called Ravinia where people from all over Chicagoland listen to concerts. We had lunch in downtown Highland Park, and as we were talking out of the blue, Ellen said, "I read that Highland Park has a thriving Jewish community and beautiful synagogues."

"You have been doing your homework," I replied with a smile.

"If we ever got married and I moved to Chicago, this is where we will live," Ellen said confidently.

I couldn't help myself and laughed out loud and said, "Then you will have to marry someone else because I can't afford to live in Highland Park. Do you know what the average cost of a house is here? Ellen, I'm not kidding, we can't afford to live here."

Ellen didn't say anything out loud but had this little smirk as if she was thinking, "Oh, we will see about that."

After giving Ellen the grand tour, we went back to my place and relaxed a bit. I knew Ellen loved wine, so I thought it would be nice if I picked up some wine for her. Well, that didn't really go as planned. Ellen said, "You bought some wine, where is it?" she asked.

"It's in the refrigerator," I responded.

Ellen quickly jumped up and ran and opened the refrigerator. Then I heard this God awful "John!!!!!!!!!!", she screamed.

"You bought me boxed wine"? I guess there are some very good quality boxed wines, but of course, that's not what I bought. I bought some cheap two-buck chuck.

Ellen just smirked and said, "I see I need to educate you on wine." That night, we went to a fun Halloween party at my dear friends Kevin and Margie's house. Ellen was dressed as a cat and looked amazingly sexy in a tight little body suit, complete with whiskers and ears, and I was dressed as Confucius. Don't ask me where I came up with that idea, but I did look rather cool. We had a great time, one of the best Halloween parties I had ever attended. Halloween was Margie's favorite holiday, and she always did it right.

The next morning, Ellen and I were very excited. We had decided it was time for her to meet Brett and Brandon. We drove to my ex-wife's house, picked up the boys, and took them to Chucky Cheese where we played games and ordered pizza and drinks. For never having been married and having no kids, I was very impressed with how natural Ellen was with the boys. As Ellen and I were getting more serious, it was important that Brett and Brandon were comfortable with Ellen and build a relationship with her over time. Of course, they were a bit shy at first, especially Brett, but after a period, they both warmed up to Ellen.

After spending the better part of the day with the boys, we dropped them back off at their mom's. It was at the drop-off when Ellen first met my Ex-wife. Happily, everyone was cordial, which was great for the boys. That evening, I treated Ellen by taking her to a John Mayer concert at the Hard Rock in downtown Chicago. The concert was awesome, and we had a great time.

Ellen and I had that in common. We liked the energy of big cities, and we both loved live music. After the concert, we started the forty-five-minute drive north, got back to Grayslake around 1:00 AM, and fell fast asleep. We didn't sleep too late into the morning as Ellen had to catch a flight back to San Diego. We got up, Ellen made me a great breakfast, and we relaxed watching the news. Sadly, it was time to take Ellen to the airport. Each time we had to say goodbye to each other became harder and harder. We had such a great time together and did not want to be a part.

Chapter 12

Now What?

Over the next four months, Ellen and I continued to take turns visiting each other, traveling back and forth between San Diego and Chicago. On one of our trips, we flew to Olean to introduce Ellen to my parents. My parents were immediately impressed with Ellen. Of course, my dad was always nice to the girls I would bring home for them to meet. On the other hand, my mother was always tougher and somewhat critical, and I think she sometimes intimidated my girlfriends.

But let me tell you, my mother met her match with Ellen. When I brought Ellen into the house, she immediately took control, and within an hour, she had my mother laughing and joking. It was really great to see. Also during our visit to western New York, we went to a Buffalo Bills game where Ellen met my friends Rob and Andrew, and we had the best time.

Our relationship was progressing extremely well. We loved spending time together and always had so much fun. As Ellen and I started to get more serious about our relationship, we began discussing marriage. We knew we loved each other but there were some topics we really needed to get aligned on. The first challenge we needed to solve was where we would live if we were to get married. To my surprise, Ellen offered to move to Chicago. She understood my children and my career were in Chicago, and there would be no way to move to San Diego, at least not at this time.

While I might be able to find a different job, there was no way I would leave my kids, especially at such a young age. Ellen worked from home, and her sales position allowed her to work anywhere in the country. Problem solved: Ellen agreed to move to Chicago but said, "At some point, you need to move us to San Diego." Afterall, her mother, sisters, and cousins were all in San Diego. I didn't know exactly how I would pull that off, but I agreed I would get her back to San Diego someday.

The next hurdle we would run into was religion. You might think the fact that I was Catholic and Ellen was Jewish would be a major barrier, but it was a topic we addressed very well together. My religious beliefs set very young and very deep, were personal. While I have always considered myself spiritual, I never really considered myself religious, and I do think there is a distinction between the two. I knew Judaism was extremely important to Ellen and her entire family. I agreed when we had children, we would raise them Jewish. Though I never promised I would convert from Catholicism to Judaism, I think deep down, Ellen and her mother hoped I would convert.

For the time being, I agreed to raise our children Jewish; I would attend synagogue, and we would have a Jewish home.

Although, as time would tell, I didn't quite understand what that meant. One of the worst arguments Ellen and I had was about Christmas. Christmas was absolutely my favorite holiday of the year. Yes, because it was a celebration of the birth of Jesus Christ; but it also had deep cultural meaning to me. It was a time of peace, family, goodwill, and celebration. I loved Christmas time — the lights, tree decor, and presents. As more time passed, I realized that to maintain a Jewish home, we would not be able to have a Christmas tree or Christmas lights in our home. We would celebrate Christmas for me in other ways, but it would need to be outside of our home.

We even consulted with our Rabbi at the time, and he stated that although many interfaith couples do celebrate both Christmas and Hannukah, it was not ideal and would be difficult for Jewish children to fully embrace their Jewish faith with multiple religious beliefs celebrated in the home. This was a real problem for me, and I knew many interfaith couples celebrated both Jewish holidays and Christian holidays. However, it was very important to Ellen that we not confuse our children with mixed messages, and I eventually agreed to those conditions.

As our discussions grew more intense, the topic of children came up, and we both learned very quickly that we had potentially hit a major challenge that might prevent us from getting married. I had been married before, I already had two children; I was getting very close to 40, and the thought of starting over was terrifying to me. On the other hand, Ellen had never been married and absolutely wanted to start a family together. Sadly, it ended up being a deal breaker. I certainly understood Ellen's perspective and felt bad; however, I really wanted to focus on Brett and Brandon. I knew in my heart that Ellen would be an amazing stepmom, and I was hoping that would be enough for her, but it clearly wasn't. After many long discussions and outright arguments, we decided we were too far apart on this issue and broke up.

We were both devastated, and extremely angry. We stopped talking and broke off all communication. I was heartbroken as I'm sure Ellen was as well. I rarely went out and certainly didn't start dating again. I focused more on my boys and my career. It was a very hard time for me. Many weeks went by, and I really started to miss Ellen. I wondered what she was doing and who she was with. Did she really move on? Did she already start dating again? I was a real mess.

I started to initiate a self-analysis. What was my issue with more children? At first, I thought it would just be too complicated. How would it impact Brett and Brandon? Did I have the energy for a baby? After many weeks of self-reflection, I concluded that I had the energy and desire to have more children and wanted it to be with Ellen. One evening, I called Ellen and said, "I have done a lot of soul searching. I love you; I want to have a life with you. I want to build a family with you if you will still have me." Ellen was so happy and said, "Yes, of course, I love you and want to have a family with you."

One thing I learned about Ellen and very much came to respect is that she always knows exactly what she wants and does what it takes to get it. She rarely settles. I have always admired that level of confidence. I found it not to be selfish, but self loving. So, when it was time for me to purchase the engagement ring, I was smart enough to know I better get Ellen's input. We started to visit multiple jewelry stores in both San Diego and Chicago. Over time, we designed the band I purchased in San Diego, and a beautiful diamond engagement ring I purchased in Chicago.

We had been dating for around six months, and Ellen wasn't sure when I would formally propose, but she knew a proposal was coming. During one of my visits to San Diego, I made plans to visit Ellen's mom to ask her for her daughter's hand in marriage. I kept this all on the down low from Ellen, even though she probably knew what I was up to. I went to Flo's apartment and admittedly was a little nervous. I felt a little silly, being thirty-nine years old and asking mom's permission, but I knew it was important to Ellen. Flo invited me in, and we sat down at her little kitchen table.

I didn't waste any time and just went for it, "Flo, I want you to know I love Ellen with all of my heart." Flo sat there listening intently. "I would like to marry Ellen, and I'm hoping you will give me your blessing," I said.

Flo looked directly at me and smiled and said, "When you have children, will you raise them Jewish, and will you have a Jewish home, because I think you know that's very important to Ellen?"

I quickly responded, "Yes, we absolutely will."

Flo reached out and touched my hand and said, "Then yes, you have my blessing."

Chapter 13

The Proposal was Far from Perfect

It was now June of 2022, about ten months since Ellen and I met. Things were coming together nicely. Now, I had to make the proposal as romantic as how we met, so I decided to book a trip to Hawaii. I suggested to Ellen that we should make a trip to Hawaii for a little getaway. Although I never announced this was the proposal trip, I think Ellen and her entire family knew what I was up to. I told Ellen I would take care of all the arrangements, and she agreed.

We would visit both Oahu and Maui. I booked the airfare and researched hotels. I didn't book the Four Seasons or anything, but the hotels I selected were nice. Ellen and her family had figured it would be during this trip I would formally pop the question. While Ellen and I were going through security at San Diego airport, I was doing my best to hide the ring so it would be a surprise, but little sneak Ellen spotted the ring as I took it out of my bag to go through an X-ray.

Ellen was watching the ring case go down the belt into the machine and had a huge smile on her face. The flight to Hawaii was just over five hours. We talked, took cat naps, and read. As soon as we stepped off the plane in Oahu, we immediately felt the warm Hawaiian air and detected the soothing scent of flowers. I had arranged for us to receive the beautiful flower leis, Hawaii is known for. As soon as we cleared the gate area, we were greeted by two beautiful Hawaiian girls wearing traditional Hawaiian sun dresses, probably twenty-one years old. They had a sign with my last name on it. When I waved to them, they walked up to us, put the leis around our necks, and said, "Aloha." Their smiles were so inviting and genuine, and the aroma of the leis was soothing. It was such a great feeling.

I said to Ellen, "You just got leid in Hawaii". I know it was cheesy, and Ellen smacked me for it, but I just couldn't resist. I rented a car so Ellen and I could explore the island. When we arrived at our hotel, we were immediately greeted by a young Hawaiian man dressed in white slacks and a button-down floral shirt. He opened the taxi door for us, and as we stepped out, another hotel representative handed us some type of tropical drink. Ah, we were in paradise. The hotel I picked was probably three or four stars. It was nice and right on the water in Waikiki. It felt great to be there, and I was looking forward to asking Ellen to marry me in such a beautiful place.

As we stepped up to the front desk for check-in, I gave my name to the young desk clerk who greeted us. He immediately found our reservation. Ellen quickly stepped up and asked, "What type of room do we have?"

"It's a beautiful room facing the ocean, madam," the clerk responded.

"Is it on a high floor? We need a very quiet room, as we are light sleepers. Is it full ocean view, or partial ocean view?" asked Ellen.

It was at that moment that I stepped back from the reservation desk and went and sat down. I watched from where I was sitting while Ellen and the clerk researched room options. About ten minutes later, Ellen came over with a huge smile and said, "I got us a much better room, bigger, with a better view, I told them it was a special occasion."

I said, "Wow, I didn't really think to tell them it was a special occasion." While I was certainly pleased to get a better room, admittedly, I felt a little put off by that exchange. After all, this was the trip I booked, made all the arrangements, and wanted it to be special for Ellen. It was as if what I planned wasn't good enough. Our time in Hawaii was quite enjoyable. After all, Hawaii is one of the most beautiful places on earth. It's hard to have a bad time in Hawaii.

During our two days on Oahu, we enjoyed the hotel, worked out in the gym, sat by the pool, enjoyed nice meals, and, of course, enjoyed some intimacy. We drove all over the island, visited Pearl Harbor, and Hanama Bay, and did a fair amount of shopping in the amazing Hawaiian markets. The people of Hawaii were warm and inviting. The weather was perfect, and the ocean was the deepest blue water I had ever seen. The entire time, I kept thinking about when the right time would be to propose to Ellen. "Should I do it here on Oahu or wait until Maui?" I'm sure Ellen was thinking the same thing.

On the third day, we checked out of our hotel, headed to the airport, and returned to the rental car. We would take a short flight over to Maui. Our hotel in Maui was very nice and we received the same royal Hawaiian treatment upon arrival as we did on the other island. I noticed that upon check-in Ellen followed the same process as she did before. She inquired about the location of the room. She asked if it was a quiet room and what floor it was on. Deep down, it absolutely made me uncomfortable, as if the proposal trip I planned did not live up to her standards. I decided to say something to Ellen about it.

I said, "Ellen, I'm getting a little upset here. I planned every detail of this trip, and you don't seem to like what I have arranged." Ellen quickly dismissed it and said, "John, I'm in sales, and I travel all the time for work. I know what I like, and I just want to make sure we have the best room possible." I didn't really like it and felt a little put off, but I just backed off and let Ellen take charge of the logistics going forward.

Just when you think it couldn't get more beautiful, as we drove around the island of Maui, Ellen and I were simply amazed at the island's natural beauty. We took the road to Hana, went up to Haleakala, a huge dormant volcano at a 10,000' elevation, and did some hiking. We visited the towns of Paia (great fish tacos), Wailea, and Kapalua. In one way, I felt Ellen, and I was connecting on many different levels. However, I found myself in a real dilemma as I was having my doubts about proposing to Ellen. It had nothing to do with love. I absolutely loved Ellen. She was perfect for me in so many ways. She was smart, beautiful, confident, high energy, and full of life. I just wasn't sure if I could keep up with her expectations for an entire lifetime. Would she be happy with me, would I be enough for her?

Our trip had come to an end, and it was time to fly back to San Diego. I did not give Ellen the ring. She was, of course, extremely upset, and we had quite an argument about it, but I said, "I'm sorry, Ellen, I'm just not sure about this, and we both need to be sure." Ellen thought I was being ridiculous. As you could imagine, the five-hour flight back to San Diego was uncomfortable, and we didn't say two words to each other. When it was time for me to head back to Chicago and Ellen and I said goodbye to each other, it was very somber.

Ellen was still very upset, and she let me know it. "How could you ask my mother for my hand in marriage, purchase the ring, plan a trip to Hawaii, let me see the ring through the X-ray machine, and not propose? I'm done!" Ellen screamed.

Ellen went on to tell me she talked with her friends and family and explained what happened in Hawaii. Everyone was of the same opinion, "Get rid of that guy. How could he do that to you?" While that was hard for me to hear, I stood my ground and told Ellen I just wasn't ready yet. That was the final straw for Ellen, and she made it clear we were over. I packed up my things, took a cab to the airport, and headed back to Chicago. I felt bad, but after the divorce I went through, I needed to make sure this was going to work before I got married again.

For the next few days, I had thought about emailing or calling Ellen, but I resisted. I had obviously hurt Ellen, and she was serious about the relationship being done. I knew I had to move on. I resumed my focus on my boys and work just as I had always done. I didn't call any old girlfriends or go out with friends. I pretty much went home after work and felt sorry for myself. I started to rethink everything. Ellen is extremely smart and confident, and she knows what she wants in life and goes after it. After all, it was she who approached me first in Venice. If she hadn't done that, I would still be standing there like a goof looking at a map of Paris. She has high expectations of herself and others around her. Those are all great qualities.

After two weeks, my heart was aching as I missed Ellen and knew I really messed up. I made up my mind. So, what if she's a little particular? "I love her, and I'm going to marry her," I said to myself. I picked up the phone and called Ellen. Fortunately, she was home, and she picked up.

"Hello, what do you want, John," Ellen said rather bluntly. I could feel the chill coming through the phone.

"Listen, things in Hawaii didn't necessarily play out as planned, and I'm sorry. We need to see each other. I want you to come to Chicago next weekend. I promise, it will be worth it," I said. I didn't make any commitments or promises. I just asked her to come visit. To my surprise, Ellen agreed.

When Ellen arrived in Chicago, it was getting late and, on the way home from the airport, we stopped at a local Grayslake restaurant and had a nice dinner before heading back to my place. Once in my townhouse, Ellen said, "I feel like taking a bath."

"Sure, go ahead," I told Ellen. I knew she loved to take baths. It was relaxing for her. I was more of a shower guy, but I did have some bubble baths for when my boys stayed over and took baths. I waited probably twenty minutes. I would hear Ellen splashing around in there, and she would occasionally turn on the water to warm it up. I couldn't take it any longer. I knocked on the door.

"Hey, do you mind if I come in?" I said sheepishly. As soon as I entered the bathroom, I could see Ellen's beautiful little body all covered in bubbles, with her pretty legs picking through the suds. Reminded me of some old Marilyn Monroe movie or something. I sat down on the floor on the side of the tub and smiled at Ellen.

"Did you want something?" Ellen said rather seductively. At that moment, I produced the engagement ring box and opened it in front of her.

I held out my hand and said, "As a matter of fact, I do want something. I love you, Ellen, and I want you to be my wife. Will you marry me?" I placed the ring on her finger, and it looked stunning. I was rather happy with myself. At that moment, Ellen popped out of the tub, wrapped herself in a towel, and ran over to the side of the bed where the phone was on the nightstand. She never told me if she would marry me or not. She dialed the phone frantically.

A few seconds later, Ellen shouted out, "Mom! I'm getting married, and I'm going to have a baby!"

I was still sitting on the floor holding the empty ring box, with my mouth wide open. "Baby, what baby? Who said anything about a baby? We just got engaged. I think we need to plan the wedding first," I said. I don't think Ellen heard me or if she did, she just ignored me. She was too busy talking to her mom. I just laughed. This was classic Ellen.

With the official proposal behind us, the wedding planning immediately commenced. We had two engagement parties: one in

Chicago, and one in San Diego. The party in Chicago was at my townhouse and I had invited some close personal friends as well as some fun co-workers from Allstate.

One of my good friends from work, Valerie, offered a toast, stood up, and said, "John, I know I told you to bring me back something from Europe, but you really outdid yourself with this," pointing to Ellen. Everyone laughed, and that was the start of a great party.

Later, in San Diego, we had a similar party with many of Ellen's friends and family, and we enjoyed an equally great time.

Chapter 14

It Never Rains in Southern California

We selected November 9th as our wedding date and sent invitations to friends and family with ample notice. We planned a relatively small wedding, about seventy guests total. Ellen and I worked together for hours trying to narrow down the guest list, which we found to be overwhelming. Ellen and her mother did extensive research on wedding locations, visiting many venues in the San Diego area. After about a month, we selected the Marriott on Coronado Island, which checked all the boxes in terms of location, price, and accommodations.

Next, we would need to select Ellen's bridesmaids and my groomsmen. Ellen was very close to her youngest sister Carole, so of course, Ellen asked her to be one of her bridesmaids. As soon as I met Carole and her husband Andrew, I knew we would be lifelong friends, in addition to being family. Next up, Ellen selected her best friend from childhood, Lena DeLuca. Lena and Ellen were inseparable growing up. We were excited because Lena and her husband Enrico would come all the way from Long Island for the wedding. And last but not least was Carol Treadway. Carol and Ellen were best friends and traveled all over as single girls having a blast together, no doubt getting themselves in trouble.

For my groomsmen, the top of my list was Andrew Luke, not only were we best of friends, but I would never have met Ellen had it not been for Andrew's coaxing me to visit Europe. My second groomsman was my good friend from Chicago, Kevin Will. Kevin and I met when we were neighbors in the northern suburbs of Chicago and became very good friends. I spent a lot of time with Kevin and his wife Margie, as they were fun-loving and always came up with new ways to have fun. My third groomsman was my good friend Rob Korody. Rob and I were roommates in college, and he also trained with me in Kung Fu, and became an outstanding martial artist.

The weekend of the wedding was finally here. Ellen was very upset as we had been watching the weather forecast and it was showing a 90% chance of rain. We had planned an outdoor wedding as the average temperature in San Diego is 73 degrees and usually sunny.

"It never rains in southern California, except the weekend of my wedding. What are we going to do?" Ellen cried out.

Ellen called the wedding coordinator at the Marriott in a panic. The wedding coordinator was amazing. She was also tracking the weather, and she had arranged to move the wedding inside and reserved one of their nicest rooms.

"Don't worry, Ellen, everything will be perfect, and your wedding will be beautiful," the woman said with complete confidence.

I was impressed with her professionalism, which somewhat put our minds at ease. Ellen and I both wanted to show our out-of-town guests how beautiful San Diego is, which added to the disappointment. We would just have to go with the flow. We picked a nice Italian restaurant in Cardiff by the Sea for our out-of-town guests for the evening before the wedding. The dinner was so much fun as it was great to host our special guests, including Ellen's cousins from Florida, and of course my parents came in from western New York, and many of my friends from Chicago.

After dinner, many of us went downtown San Diego to hit the nightlife. The girls went their way, and the guys went another way. Lena's husband Enrico was the ringleader for setting up my impromptu bachelor party. Enrico, a smart, confident, fun loving New Yorker took charge. We started hitting one bar after another, and every place we went, Enrico ordered a round of tequila shots. We had an amazing time. After a couple of hours and way too many shots of tequila, we took taxis back to the hotel. Let me tell you from experience, I don't recommend having your bachelor party the night before the wedding.

It was the morning of the wedding. I begrudgingly opened my eyes but knew that I would need to get up and get moving. My mouth was dry, and my head was pounding. One by one, my groomsmen came in to check on me. At one point, I was feeling so badly, I said to the guys, "I don't think I'm going to make it to the wedding."

Without hesitation, they all jumped into action. Andrew brought me water, Kevin produced Tylenol, and Bob made me jump in the shower and turned the water to freezing cold. I was screaming in agony as the guys were all laughing their asses off. After about an hour, I managed to pull myself together.

It was an hour before the wedding, and we were growing concerned as we had not received any word from the two musicians we had booked to play music during the wedding ceremony. We could not imagine what had happened as we booked them months in advance and even gave them a down payment.

The Marriott wedding coordinator called Ellen and said softly, "Ellen, I got in touch with your musicians, and they made a major mistake and went to the wrong address. They got their bookings mixed up and ended up going to LA, and there is no way they are going to make it here in time. But listen, don't worry, I have the best wedding soundtrack on tape, and we will use that. Trust me, it will work beautifully."

Ellen called me, was extremely upset, and cried, "John, first we had a torrential downpour the day of my wedding, now we won't have our musicians."

I said, "El, it will be fine. Our guests are not here for the weather, they are here to celebrate our marriage, and the music is going to be perfect. Our wedding planner knows exactly what to do, so let's just have a wonderful wedding and reception."

That seemed to provide Ellen a little comfort, and she whimpered, "Ok, I love you."

As the wedding time approached, things started to get more settled. Ellen and her bridesmaids were getting hair and makeup done and getting dressed. We hired a very talented hair and makeup professional for the girls. In our own special way, me and the boys got ready as well. Andrew helped Brett and Brandon get their tuxes on and attached the corsage. They looked so handsome. One by one, each of the guys came into my room, all dressed in their tuxes. Everyone looked awesome.

At the time designated, we proceeded to a separate room next to the wedding chamber per the planner's instructions. The guys were all very supportive and full of jokes and smiles, as can be expected with men. "You sure you want to do this (again)?" someone said.

"There's still time to sneak out the back door" another shouted out. My head was still pounding from the tequila the night before, and I was still very much hung-over, but I knew I needed to pull it together.

It was almost time for the wedding to start, and I was very nervous. However, it gave me great comfort to have such good friends with me during this very special time. Andrew and his beautiful wife Julia flew in all the way from Toronto, Kevin and

Margie came in from Illinois, and Bob came in from New York. My heart was full.

The wedding planner popped her head in and said, "Ok, all of the guests are seated, it's time for us to go, follow me." She took us to the hallway just outside of the wedding chamber, where Ellen's bridesmaids were already waiting for us. Of course, Ellen was nowhere in sight, hidden in a special room somewhere, I assumed. Things then moved very quickly, all well-choreographed by the wedding planner. I put my arm around Brett and proceeded into the wedding chamber while all our guests turned back and looked on with warm smiles. There was a beautiful white carpet that went all the way from the back of the room right to the front of the room where the Rabbi was standing under the beautiful Chuppah, the Jewish wedding canopy where Ellen and I would take our vows together.

I led Brett to the front row and had him sit next to my mother and father, who were already seated, and went to take my place by the Rabbi. The Rabbi must have sensed my nervousness and said calmly with a big smile, "Relax, John, all of these wonderful people are here to celebrate you and Ellen. Just enjoy it." I really liked Rabbi Coskey. Since I wasn't Jewish, we had difficulty finding a Rabbi that would marry us, unless I converted to Judaism. After an extensive search and being turned down by several Rabbis in the San Diego area, we found Rabbi Coskey, who met with us for a long period of time, and after understanding we were committed to having a Jewish home, she agreed to marry us.

I noticed the room was quite spectacular, and I immediately thought the wedding planner had come through for us. The music she selected was perfect; the scent of fresh flowers filled the air, and the lighting was just right. As I scanned the room, I could see all our dear friends sitting there, it was a wonderful feeling. At that moment, the music changed, and I knew the wedding was beginning. Usually very calm under pressure, I was extremely nervous, and my legs were locked in place as if I couldn't move. I was just praying I wouldn't pass out as a side effect from the tequila. I knew I needed to just relax and enjoy the amazing experience, so I used my martial arts experience to calm my mind.

Carol and Rob entered the room next and walked slowly to take their places on each side. Well timed out, Lena and Kevin entered the room, followed by Carol and Andrew. Then the cute show began as Ellen's niece Megan came in dropping flower petals from a beautiful cloth bag (Megan is Ellen's sister Gwen's youngest daughter). Megan was partnered with my son Brandon who was all smiles carrying the ring pillow. They were adorable together.

***Our niece Megan was our flower girl and
son Brandon was the ring bearer***

The music changed again, and I knew I would finally get a chance to see my beautiful bride-to-be. Suddenly, Ellen and her mother appeared in the doorway and slowly walked down the aisle. All the guests quickly stood and turned around as usual. As Ellen walked down the aisle, I became emotional. She was absolutely stunning in her beautiful strapless, ankle length wedding gown, a shapely design which complimented her athletic figure. She wore elegant white gloves that went just below the elbow and a gorgeous necklace. Her smile lit up the room and it reminded me of the first day we met in St. Mark's Square. Ellen was holding her mother's arm. Florence looked quite beautiful herself, wearing all smiles and beaming with pride.

Ellen seated her mother in the front row and took her place by me, and the Rabbi turned us first towards each other, then to face our guests. I immediately noticed Brett and Brandon sitting in the front row, both smiling from ear to ear. Rabii Coskey then welcomed everyone and began to tell the story of how Ellen and I met.

"I spent quality time with Ellen and John in preparation for today's ceremony. You see, the story of how they met is quite exceptional, and wanted to share this with you all today. John, living in Chicago at the time, was backpacking through Europe by himself. Ellen was vacationing in Europe with two of her girlfriends. While in Venice, Italy, Ellen was standing in front of a gift shop near St. Mark's Square and saw this guy walk by and thought to herself, 'My, my, that guy has a nice butt'."

***A man is truly blessed when his wife looks at him this
way***

Everyone in the audience laughed out loud and my sons were chuckling. "At that moment, John turned around and saw that Ellen was smiling at him. He didn't know what to do and just froze, so he reached into his backpack and pulled out a map as if he was lost, turns out it was a map of Paris. Ellen made the first move and approached John and introduced herself; the rest of the story brings us all here today".

I was quite impressed as that was a great way to break the ice and set a positive tone for the ceremony.

The rest of the wedding was equally special. We had decided we wanted the ceremony to be relatively short. The Rabbi said several prayers, including very loving best wishes for our life together. We exchanged rings, and we were announced, man and wife. Ellen and I embraced and gave each other a loving kiss.

At the end of the ceremony, I broke the traditional glass with my foot. The room was full of smiles and happy tears. The music shifted again with a tone of energy and happiness. The wedding party exited the room as they had entered, arm and arm in pairs, followed by Ellen and me. We were then escorted by the wedding planner to a separate room, where we waited for our guests to enter the reception hall and get situated.

When Ellen and I walked in, all our guests were already there, and we were greeted by applause and cheers. It was a very happy moment for us. Ellen and her mom did a great job selecting the reception, as the setting was beautiful, and the food was outstanding. The wedding court sat at the head table. We really felt quite honored. As soon as all were seated, the drinks began to flow along with appetizers. One by one, each of the bridesmaids and groomsmen made their speeches, which were both moving and hilarious.

After the speeches concluded, it was time to kick off the dancing segment of the reception. First, it was time for the garter removal. A chair was strategically placed in the center of the dance floor where Ellen was seated. She looked stunning in her beautiful gown. Playing to the crowd, she pulled her dress up slightly and crossed her gorgeous legs, revealing the sexy little garter. The cheering and clapping commenced, and I kneeled in front of my lovely bride and ran my hands up her thighs to the garter as the guests yelled, "You go John." Always the ham; instead of removing the garter with my hands, I removed it with my teeth as the crowd roared louder.

Next the DJ ordered all the single guys to the floor for the garter toss. The music grew louder, and the clapping started. I turned and launched the garter, and to my surprise, it was my buddy Rob who leaped up in the air like a jaguar. It was surprising because, as the myth goes, the man who catches the garter will be the next one to marry, and Rob is the least likely to get married.

Now, it was Ellen's turn. She quickly stood up and the wedding planner handed Ellen the bouquet, and the DJ coaxed the single ladies in the room to the dance floor. Ellen turned, the energy in the room was intense, as Ellen threw the bouquet over her shoulder. I have never seen anything like it, as it was a free-for-all. The bouquet hit the floor, and five girls jumped on it like a fumbled football in the NFL. I don't know who came up with the bouquet.

Next, the DJ began to play some high energy music, and before you knew it, most everyone was out on the dance floor. We enjoyed all the traditional Jewish wedding rituals, including the

Hora and hoisting Ellen and me up on chairs. I was terrified they would drop us or smash our heads on the ceiling, but we managed to survive, and it was so much fun. It was important to Ellen and me that we spent time at the reception with our guests, so we divided and conquered. Ellen took one side of the room, and I took the other. We did this periodically through dinner and while people were dancing. It was great catching up with everyone, albeit just briefly, as we circulated around the hall. I loved seeing my parents out on the dance floor, having a wonderful time as if they were young again. Brett and Brandon were having a great time, dancing with family members, and hamming it up on the dance floor.

Ellen was very close to her cousin Andrea, and their young boys were very talented entertainers. Andrea had arranged for her son Alex, ten years old, to sing us a song during the reception. There wasn't a dry eye in the house. This young man was quite talented. Ellen's Uncle Dave, accompanied by his sister Florence (Ellen's mom), led the Jewish prayer for bread (Motzi).

After more eating, drinking, and dancing, it was time for the cake. Since Ellen's favorite dessert was cheesecake, we decided to have a local bakery make our wedding cake a magnificent three-tier cheesecake. Before our guests were served, Ellen and I conducted the traditional cut of the cake, and there was a slight smush on the face but nothing too crazy. We danced, ate, and sang the night away, enjoying every minute with friends and family.

***From L-R: Rob, Andrew, Kevin, John, Ellen, Carol,
Lena, Ellen's sister Carole; and Brandon and Brett***

After the wedding, we planned to stay in San Diego for a couple of days before leaving for our honeymoon in Spain. It didn't take long for us to experience our first real marital challenge, as Ellen could not find her passport anywhere. We turned her condo upside down and even had her mother come over to help, but that passport was nowhere to be found. We kept our cool and arranged to travel up to Los Angeles, where we would get an emergency passport. It delayed our honeymoon by a couple of days, but we got through it. We had a wonderful honeymoon exploring Madrid and

Seville. It was the perfect way to begin our life together.

With the wedding behind us, Ellen and I turned our focus on finding our home. Ellen hired a realtor and put her townhouse on the market. San Diego real estate was very hot, and the townhouse sold within weeks for a very nice profit. We then hired a realtor in Chicago, someone who was experienced in North Shore properties. He would first help us sell my townhouse in Grayslake while helping us find our new home. I continued to try to convince Ellen there would be no way for us to afford a home in Highland Park, even with the money she and I made on the sale of our townhomes.

Ellen pretty much dismissed my concerns and instructed our realtor to find us the diamond in the rough house close to our price range, preferably in Highland Park. Things seem to come together nicely with my townhouse selling first. Ellen was still spending most of her time in San Diego until her condo transaction was completed. I was back in Chicago working and looking for our perfect home. Our realtor showed us multiple properties on the north shore, but everything was either too old and needed too much work or too expensive.

We were touring one home that we both thought was perfect for us. We spent a lot of time going through every inch of the house. Just as we were about to discuss putting in an offer, the house began to shake as the train tracks were not too far behind the house, something the realtor either didn't know or neglected to tell us. "Next," Ellen shouted out. Then, a couple of weeks later, our realtor called and said, "You two must see this little gem of a house I found in Highland Park. It's just perfect for you."

We picked a time when Ellen was going to be in Chicago, and we scheduled a time to see the house. As we drove into the neighborhood, we were already happy. The house was situated on Dell Lane, a quiet beautiful street walking distance to Ravinia Music Festival. We pulled up to the house and we both looked at each other and smiled. It was a cute little 1930 house with three bedrooms, two baths, 1800 square feet with great curb appeal, a nice front yard with an old oak tree that provided shade for the house, which looked like it had been well maintained over the years.

The house had a living room and dining room visible as you just walk into the house. The kitchen was small but was all upgraded, and off the kitchen was a sitting room with a gorgeous bay window facing the front yard. The basement had a nice, finished basement with a big bedroom, which would be perfect for when Brett and Brandon stayed over. Upstairs was the master bedroom and another room, perfect for a baby's room someday. This was going to be our new home. We put down an offer that day and bought the house, after some swift negotiating from Ellen.

Ellen headed back to San Diego to take care of business there while I closed on selling my townhome and purchasing the house in Highland Park. With so much going on, the holidays seemed to fly by and the next thing we knew it was January 2003. After a while, it became obvious Ellen was stalling moving to Chicago. Her condo sale was finalized, but she wasn't making any concrete plans to move. While I understood it wasn't going to be easy moving from sunny San Diego to cold Chicago in January, I said, "Babe, we are married now. Your home is here in Highland Park."

I even called her mother and said, "Flo, can you help me get your daughter's tush on a plane and send here to Chicago?" A couple of weeks later, Ellen finally arrived and got settled in. It wasn't long at all before Ellen felt quite at home. We joined a beautiful Synagogue, North Shore Congregation Israel. The people of Highland Park welcomed us with open arms, and we quickly developed wonderful friendships.

Chapter 15

Our Little Gift from God

As we were getting settled into our new home in Highland Park and both back to work, Ellen wasted no time turning her attention to having a baby. "You know, John, I'm at the age where I can't wait too long before we start our family together," Ellen said.

To which I promptly responded, "Babe, we just got married, let's enjoy our time, just you and I, before the kids come along; I'm thinking we can start trying in a year or two."

"Yah, well, uh no, it may take a year or two, or longer to get pregnant, we should start now," Ellen stated very matter-of-factly. Reminded me of the movie My Cousin Vinny when Marisa Tomei stomped her foot and said, "My biological clock is ticketing." And so, the project to get pregnant was underway. Please understand, I thoroughly enjoyed the work involved, mind you, but Ellen was clearly on a mission, which included various sure fire pregnancy strategies, and post-intercourse positions to optimize egg fertilization. It was quite hysterical, and sure enough, two months later, Ellen was pregnant. Let me tell you, when that girl has her mind set on something, even mother-nature is afraid to disappoint her.

After the first trimester and multiple encouraging doctor's

appointments, we announced the pregnancy to friends and family. A new project was then initiated: to prepare the baby's room. Ellen was in full nesting mode and drove me crazy. I painted the baby's room three times, and it still wasn't right. I told Ellen, "Sweetie, I love you, but I'm not painting that room again."

"Fine, I will call a professional painter then," she responded with no hesitation. Within a couple of months, the baby's room was perfectly painted, the baby would have a top-of-the-line crib and changing table, and the mom would have a beautiful rocking chair. The pregnancy glow is a real thing. Ellen seemed to be just beaming all the time.

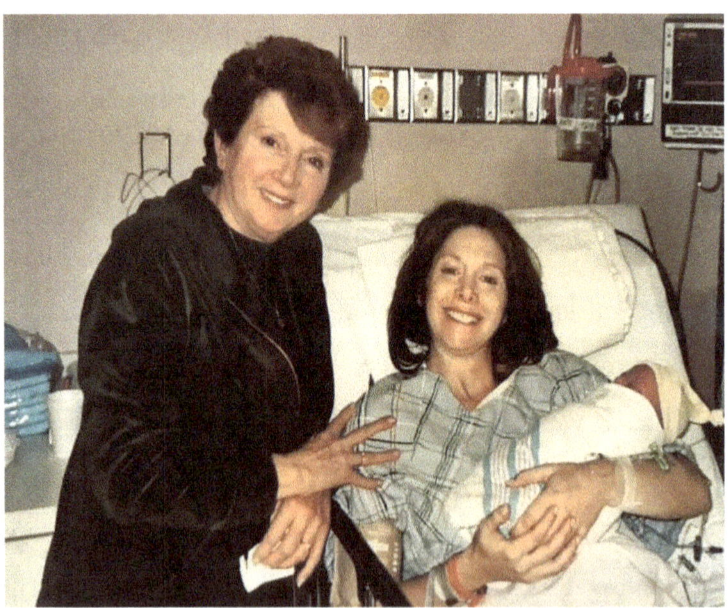

Grandma Flo, Ellen, and baby Ethan

Exactly eleven months after we started trying to get pregnant, Ellen gave birth to our little boy on October 28th, and we named him Ethan Harrison after Ellen's grandfather Harry, as Jewish traditions suggest. Ethan was the cutest little baby, with perfect features, brilliant green eyes, and a beautiful smile like his mother. While I knew Ellen loved me with all her heart, the birth of Ethan was everything to her. Ellen transitioned to motherhood quite naturally, and I knew she would be a wonderful mother.

It seemed like my life was now complete. I had a promising career, I had my two special boys, Brett and Brandon, I found my life partner, and Ethan was our little gift from God. I was grateful for my blessings and looked confidently towards my future. I thought to myself, "None of this would have been possible, if not for that Venice smile".

The End

Postscript

At the time of publication, Ellen and John are happily married and have made their home in the northern suburbs of San Diego since 2008. On their eleventh wedding anniversary, Ellen and John renewed their marriage vows in Venice, and Ethan was by their side. Brett is happily married and proudly serving in the United States Air Force stationed at the Little Rock Air Force Base. Brandon is a graduate of California State University, Chico, where he studied Business Finance; and makes his home in the San Diego area. Ethan is a student at California Polytechnic State University in San Luis Obispo studying business. Grandma Flo, now 85 years old, lives with Ellen and John and is the best grandma anyone could ever ask for. Sadly, John's mom passed away in 2018, but John moved his dad, now 94, to San Diego, and they see each other often. Ellen and John are still very close to their wedding party, although admittedly would love to see them more often.